CARTER
HEYWARD

WHEN BOUNDARIES BETRAY US

THE PILGRIM PRESS   CLEVELAND, OHIO

The Pilgrim Press, Cleveland, Ohio 44115
© 1993 by Carter Heyward
Foreword and Preface © 1999 by Carter Heyward

Acknowledgment is made for the following: Poetry © 1984 by Audre Lorde, excerpted from the essay "Age, Race, Sex, and Class," *Sister Outsider*, The Crossing Press, Freedom, CA. An excerpt from "On Lies, Secrets and Silence" by Adrienne Rich ©1979 by W. W. Norton & Company, Inc.

Printed in the United States of America on acid-free paper

04   03   02   01   00   99   5   4   3   2   1

Library of Congress Cataloging-in-Publication Data

Heyward, Carter.
    When boundaries betray us / Carter Heyward ; foreword by Roy SteinhoffSmith ; afterword by Janet L. Surrey.
        p.   cm.
    Originally published: 1st ed. San Francisco, Calif. :
HarperSanFrancisco, c1993 with subtitle: Beyond illusions of what is ethical in therapy and life.
    Includes bibliographical references.
    ISBN 0-8298-1347-0 (acid-free paper)
    1. Psychotherapy—Moral and ethical aspects—Case studies.
    2. Psychotherapist and patient—Case studies.   I. Title.
RC480.8.H48   1999
174'.2—dc21

                                                    99-41289
                                                         CIP

In loving memory
of Audre Lorde (1934-1992)

I dedicate this book
to my teacher, the incomparable Betty Smith Broder,
my remarkable mother, Mary Ann,
and all the sisters
trying to heal
together

Women have to think whether we want, in our relationships with each other, the kind of power that can be obtained through lying.

Women have been driven mad, "gaslighted," for centuries by the refutation of our experience and our instincts in a culture which validates only male experience. The truth of our bodies and our minds has been mystified to us. We therefore have a primary obligation to each other: not to undermine each other's sense of reality for the sake of expediency; not to gaslight each other.

Women have often felt insane when cleaving to the truth of our experience. Our future depends on the sanity of each of us, and we have a profound stake, beyond the personal, in the project of describing our reality as candidly and fully as we can to each other.

Adrienne Rich,
On Lies, Secrets, and Silence

Contents

Foreword (1999)

Roy Herndon SteinhoffSmith

IN MODERN WESTERN SERVICE economies, in which helping professionals are a privileged elite, clients constitute an oppressed class:

> The power to label people deficient and declare them in need is the basic tool of control and oppression in modern industrialized societies of democratic and totalitarian persuasions. The agents with comprehensive power in these societies are the helping professionals. Their badge bestows the caring authority to declare their fellow citizens "clients"— a class of deficient people in need.[1]

In this book, Carter Heyward, by writing as a client, starts a revolution. "Revolutions begin when people who are defined as problems achieve the power to redefine the problem."[2] Heyward redefines the problem in her therapy. Her psychiatrist and the critical reviewers of this book define her, the client, as the problem.[3] She counters that the problem lay in the suffering she and her psychiatrist inflicted on each other, under the influence of heretofore largely unexamined ideologies about "what is ethical in therapy" (to quote the original subtitle of this book). She traces the sources of this suffering to her psychiatrist's "power to label" her "deficient" and "in need," and to her own collusion in this injuring control.[4]

In modern industrialized societies, all of us are, at one time or another, clients. We are children needing education, we get sick and seek medical help, we become unemployed, we suffer and seek counseling, we retire, we seek a lawyer for help with legal difficulties, we worship and are served by a minister—in each of these and other turns, we become clients, objects of professionals' defining scrutiny. Status as a client unites the corporate executive who retains a lawyer with the unemployed single mother visited by a social worker.

Most of us do not experience our solidarity in the oppression we share in the professional service economy because, as clients, we have not achieved our power to define ourselves and the problems that afflict us. When we become clients, we tend to assume that we are the problems, even if we don't know quite how. We seek professionals who will define exactly what our problems are and how to resolve them. We become the objects of the professional exercise of power.

If, as clients, we begin to become aware of our knowledge and power and if we are privileged in other ways, our professional caretakers immediately tend to identify us as potential members of the professional elite. We enter professional schools. Years later, we emerge, as professionals, usually having disconnected our insights from their source in our experiences of suffering. We think that these insights become true, valuable, and valid only if they are translated into a body of professional expertise. After all, "a little knowledge is a dangerous thing," we as professionals (who presumably know a great deal) tell ourselves as clients (who presumably know little). In other words, we replicate, in ourselves and our personal histories, the relationship between a needy, ignorant, and deficient client and a skilled, knowledgeable, and able expert.

If, on the other hand, we, as clients who are becoming aware of our knowledge and power, are not privileged or if we resist being co-opted into the professional class, professionals attempt to return us to our "places" as passive, dependent objects by damning us as "ignorant," "pathological," "dysfunctional," or "criminal." When Heyward wrote *When Boundaries Betray Us* as a client, she opened herself to this condemnation. And it came, from a gaggle of professional and academic critics.[5]

Heyward explicitly rejects the portrayal of her psychiatrist as abusive and herself as a victim because such a portrayal tends to obscure both what was good about the relationship between them—its mutuality—and the cause of her suffering—the violent patriarchal ethic that afflicted both of them (see pages 177–78). However, in the light of her critics' denial or trivialization of Heyward's suffering and the part her psychiatrist played in it, I think it is essential to realize that Heyward's psychiatrist violated American Psychological Association ethical standards when she did not respect Heyward's right "to terminate therapy at any time," when her actions directly inflicted "pain and suffering" on Heyward, and when—as a result of her interpretation of the therapy as a battle for control, which she would not let Heyward win—she breached the commonly accepted "demonstrable standard of care."[6]

In other words, according to common and professional understandings of the word, Heyward's psychiatrist professionally abused her. These critics' failure to recognize this abuse and the suffering it caused Heyward is directly linked to their failure to recognize clients as an oppressed and therefore potentially revolutionary class. When they seek to explain these failures, the critics unintentionally mobilize the primary ideologies that elites use to rationalize oppression. They tacitly define clients (as other elites have defined people of color, women, the poor, and gays and lesbians) as members of a different, lesser species, who are inherently dependent upon professionals for nurturing, discipline, and moral guidance. Clients who accept this dependency are innocent. Clients who assert their own (in this view, illusory) knowledge and agency subvert and abuse the moral order that secures their own and others' safety.

When Heyward wrote *When Boundaries Betray Us* as a knowledgeable and powerful client, her critics did not accept this self-definition. Some maintained the view that she was a dependent "client" (though a "difficult" one—one therapist who read the book called her "the client from hell") who did not have the requisite knowledge to be commenting on the ethics of therapy[7] or who was suffering from a severe transference neurosis and whose knowledge was therefore delusional.[8] Others ignored her position as a client, instead portraying her as "dangerous" and "abusive."[9]

These views dismiss the very possibilities that Heyward and other clients suffer oppression or are revolutionary agents. One can be oppressed, this argument goes, but not as a client. That which characterizes oppression in other groups—enforced dependency, denied agency, powerlessness—is simply the way things are and should be for clients. If clients aren't agents, they certainly can't be revolutionaries. According to this view, Heyward is wrong in labeling as unethical and hurtful her psychiatrist's rightful exercise of moral control over the therapy. Such discipline is simply necessary to protect clients from their own dangerous and pathological impulses.

Heyward's book is a revolutionary case study of her resistance to these oppressive ideologies. It is about her assertion, loss, and recovery of her knowledge and power as a client. Heyward does not abandon this oppressed social location, or the incisive insights that she knows only from there. She refuses to be co-opted into the professional class, even though, as a professor of theology, she is also a member of it. She does not center herself in this privileged identity. She does not deny it, but she places the knowledge and power that her privilege gives her in the service of her work as a client to liberate herself.

Heyward began her therapy by asserting her mutual power in relation to her psychiatrist, to whom she gives the pseudonym "Elizabeth Farro." At first, Farro affirmed Heyward's knowledge and power to shape the therapy. But, as Heyward moved, logically and inevitably, into a discussion of what for her is the ethical norm for such a mutual relation, friendship, the psychiatrist became extremely ambivalent.

Hurt by Farro's rejections of the possibility of a friendship after the end of therapy, Heyward suggested that it was time to end the therapy. At this point, the psychiatrist accused Heyward of acting "unilaterally" and intimated that she needed to stay in therapy because of hidden childhood trauma (pp. 75–77). Faced with Farro's resistance to discussing termination and with this suggestion of hidden abuse, Heyward acquiesced in the psychiatrist's tacit definition of her as "a wounded, obedient child who needed to be taken care of" (p. 87) and judged her own prior assertions of her power in and knowledge about the relation to be "crazy" and "pathological."

From this point on, the therapy became a nightmare. Having renounced her own knowledge and experience, Heyward was subject to Farro's expectations. She unconsciously transformed memories of minor abuse as a child into the traumatic violations the psychiatrist sought. Significantly, in these recovered "memories," abuse and the resulting suffering emerged as a reaction to her having been "too pushy" (pp. 91–93). The "memories" expressed Heyward's subjugated knowledge of the therapy as a relation in which Farro punished her for asserting her power, but they also disguised this knowledge and so protected Heyward from the psychiatrist's punishment.

The protection failed. Heyward could not and did not wholly renounce her "pushiness." Caught in ambivalence, Farro provoked Heyward. When Heyward responded by asserting her understanding of what was happening in the therapy, the psychiatrist attacked her, not physically, but emotionally (pp. 94-95). Heyward closes the book with a discussion of how, after the therapy ended and with the help of friends, she recovered from the injury she experienced in the therapy by affirming what she and Farro had discounted— the truth of her own experience as a client.

In this book, Heyward overcomes the oppressive definition of herself as an ignorant client. In so doing, she opens other clients, which means all of us in the current American service economy, to the possibility of revolutionary awareness and activity. She introduces us to the knowledge, value, and power that lie hidden in our existence as clients, in our suffering and need and oppression. To read this book is to know that when, as a client, student, parishioner, or patient, I enter a doctor's, lawyer's, minister's, teacher's, or therapist's office, I am a powerful, knowledgeable, and responsible co-creator. I do not and should not have to relinquish my power and knowledge, especially when I am suffering and am seeking help. I do not and should not have to be subject to oppression in order to meet my needs.

Heyward demonstrates three movements that must take place for clients to achieve power: from condescension by the therapist to mutuality between therapist and client; from a world of rigidly bounded units organized around a single source of commodified power, knowledge, and goodness to a world constructed by plural subjects in relation; and from interpreting reality to changing it.

Responding to feminist critics of *When Boundaries Betray*

Us, Heyward defines what I call condescension[10] as the primary
ideology of caring professionals:

> In their commitment to end sexual exploitation, many feminist profes-
> sionals, whether or not they intend this, are lending uncritical support
> to traditionally structured dyadic relationships between a (usually male)
> expert and a less knowledgeable, less powerful, and/or less healthy (of-
> ten female) person....This quintessential professional relationship trans-
> parently reflects, and supports, white western men's assumption that
> an unchanging power-over relationship is the optimal resource for
> psychospiritual and physical healing. This arrogance, I submit, is the root
> of sexual and other forms of professional exploitation.[11]

Condescending professionals define "care" as what someone with power, knowledge, and value does for someone who lacks
power, knowledge, and value.[12] For Heyward's pastoral professional
critics, the tacit model for the caring professional is the omnipo-
tent, omniscient, and all-loving God who defines and enforces the
rules of the relation with all creatures.[13] One of Heyward's critics,
Marie Fortune, cites as a divine manifestation "the moment that the
caring surgeon's knife pierces the flesh of the patient."[14] As this
example shows, condescension is oppressive in that it establishes
as a normative end a relation in which one person treats another as
an object, rather than as a subject. It equates greater power with
sole possession of truth and what is good, and less power with the
lack of truth and what is good.[15] For instance, Fortune claims that,
because they have less power than professionals, clients also are
lacking in moral agency, the knowledge and ability necessary to
make moral decisions.[16]

The metaphor condescending professionals most commonly
use to describe the care they give is parenting. But condescension
distorts the reality of parenting in ways Heyward describes. When
Heyward acquiesced in her psychiatrist's condescension, she experienced herself as a wholly dependent, passive, wounded, and dis-
abled child. This subjugation could not be accomplished without

her sacrifice of the divine child "Sophie," the wise, assertive, and active holy manifestation who challenged the powers that afflicted Heyward (p. 93). Condescending parents implicitly require the sacrifice of their children's knowledge and agency. These parents thus deny the primary purpose of parenting, which is the nurturing of children's abilities. In a similar way, condescending professionals deny the primary purpose of healing, which is to help an injured person participate in reality in the fullest way, as a valued, co-creative agent.

In *When Boundaries Betray Us,* Heyward exposes and deconstructs the therapeutic ethic of condescension. When she accepted Farro's condescension, she did not heal; rather, she became mired in affliction, oppression, and self-alienation. Healing became possible only when she recovered her ability to assert herself as a mutual participant in the therapy. While this assertion led the psychiatrist to punish her, the resulting suffering was preferable to the affliction of being a helpless "child," powerless to know or do anything about her suffering. When she recovered her power as a mutual agent in the therapy, Heyward came to know the causes of her affliction and could take the actions necessary—for instance, terminating therapy with Farro and working with friends—to address the causes of her suffering. Heyward demonstrates that healing is a revolutionary activity in which those whose agency has been denied achieve their power to co-create reality. Healing requires a movement by the therapist from condescension to mutuality.

Condescension presumes and constructs a world of rigidly bounded units organized around a single source of commodified power, knowledge, and value. This world emerges most clearly in discussions of abuse. Condescending professionals define abuse as the violation of an individual's boundaries. In this view, an abuser breaks into and uses the victim's being for his or her own purposes. Abuse is a kind of robbery. The abuser steals what rightfully belongs to the victim, his or her control over her own body and feelings. In this world, power, knowledge, and moral agency are reified quantities—commodities. Some people possess more power, knowledge, and moral agency than other people. In this view, this unequal distribution is a brute and relatively stable fact of life.[17]

While, in this circumscribed world, abuse is a result of the unequal distribution of power, in that the person with greater power violates a person with less power, so is healing. Healing requires power, knowledge, and agency—that which, in this world, a victim lacks.[18] Healing, in this view, is a restoration by the powerful of the boundaries of the powerless. Such restoration does not redress the brute reality of inequality. Rather, the healer is like a lord who uses his power to protect his powerless serfs from further violations by other, marauding, lords.

In this world, the crucial ethical issue is the management of superior power. An ethical "lord" uses "his" power to protect, heal, and care for the weak. An unethical "lord" violates the weak, while serving "his" own needs, desires, and interests. The key to ethical behavior is thus self-abnegation, the renunciation of one's needs, desires, and interests in relation to the weak.[19]

Such ethical renunciation requires the maintenance of clear boundaries of three kinds. The ethical "lord" must construct a strict boundary between "himself" and the weak. "He" may not treat the weak as like "himself." With the weak, who are defined by their needs and desires, "he" must be pure and selfless, without needs and desires; "he" must seek only to serve.[20]

This boundary between "himself" and the weak requires the maintenance of a second boundary, between relations with the weak and relations with peers. The two spheres require different ethics. The selfless ethic governs relations with the weak. With peers, the ethical "lord" may practice an egalitarian ethic. Only with people with equal power can "he" meet "his" needs and gratify "his" desires.[21]

Maintaining these social boundaries requires the construction and maintenance of clear and firm internal boundaries. The ethical "lord" must differentiate between those impulses to action that are pure, that grow solely out of a perception of the other's need, and those that are impure, governed by one's own desires and needs. Since the body is the source of desire and need, one must maintain strict control over the body and the fantasies through which it seduces one.[22]

The world of condescension is a dualistic one. A transcendent, spiritual center purifies the power and knowledge that flow outward from it, into the embodied, material world ruled by corrupting desire and need. "Lords" or professionals occupy the next ring out from this center. Because they have access to the purified knowledge and power of the center, they possess both moral agency and the capacity to heal. Beyond the ring of the "lords" dwell two sorts of people: the weak, including clients, who, because of their distance from the center, lack the requisite power, knowledge, agency, and purity to be able to participate in ethical discussions or to make moral decisions; and fallen "lords," those potential or actual abusers who retain their superior power but have been seduced by their desires away from the rule of the purifying center. These heterodox renegades violate the boundaries through which the good "lords" protect the innocent weak.

In this world, one cannot both be a client and be knowledgeable, powerful, and ethical. If one is knowledgeable and powerful, one is ethical only if one renounces one's needs and desires in relation to the weak and is in harmony with the spiritual center, represented by the other "lords" of the inner circle. If one is knowledgeable and powerful, does not renounce one's desires in relation to the weak, and is not in harmony with the other ethical "lords," then one is a renegade "lord," a threat to the sacred and moral order.

Within this world of condescension, Heyward's account is

incomprehensible. She does not present herself as an innocent or powerless client or victim of therapy. Rather, she describes herself as a powerful and knowledgeable participant who is complicit in her own affliction. She does not present her psychiatrist as a renegade "lord" who used her for her own ends. Rather, she describes her psychiatrist as injuring her in an attempt to maintain the clear boundaries required by the condescending professional ethic. In Heyward's description, the psychiatrist was also a victim of an inherently oppressive and abusive condescending order.

In order to accept Heyward's account, the reader must reject the world organized around a unitary center. Heyward's knowledge and power as a client are different from Farro's. This difference is precisely what the psychiatrist and the critics cannot accept. Caught in condescension, they conceive only one source of power, knowledge, and morality. And so, for instance, Marie Fortune dismisses Heyward's book with the comment that Heyward is ignorant of professionals' discussions of therapeutic ethics. Fortune appears unable to conceive the possibility that Heyward's different knowledge as a client might contribute to such discussions.[23]

When Boundaries Betray Us reveals that therapy is oppressive when the therapist, in the thrall of a centralized and unitary conception of reality, seeks to maintain his or her effectiveness by constructing rigid boundaries that prevent him or her from entering into a mutual relation with a client. These boundaries hurt both client and therapist in that they prevent the establishment of a relation in which each can confirm the other as different and unique, and as needed, desired, valued, knowledgeable, and powerful. Such condescending therapy is an implicit or explicit "war" in which the therapist seeks to impose his or her "healing truth" on the client. The therapist interprets the client's resistance and difference, rooted in the client's reality as a mutual participant in the therapy, as pathological, signs of illness that must be skillfully attacked and destroyed.

The therapist equates success with eliminating such resistance and so incorporating the client into the therapist's image of reality.

Such a centralized and unitary ideology rests on oppressive, but concealed, contradictions. Underlying the therapeutic ideology that Heyward exposes is the contradiction between the conception of an individual as a rigidly bounded source of whatever illness or pathology he or she experiences and the conception of healing as the incorporation of the client into a centralized, unitary, universal, and homogeneous reality. This ideology both assumes and negates boundaries. Belief in an undifferentiated and unbounded, universal reality underlies Farro's conviction that she, the psychiatrist, knew the childhood causes of Heyward's suffering. This belief led her to reject Heyward's different knowledge about this suffering. In Farro's view, certain symptoms, which Heyward displayed, indicate a childhood history of traumatic violation; and so she went looking for such traumatic events in Heyward's history, even when Heyward stated that she did not remember such severe abuse (p. 76). On the other hand, belief in the individual as a rigidly bounded unit convinced Farro that when Heyward suddenly did "remember" being severely abused, she was recovering "memories" of actual incidents in her individual history. This second belief concealed the possibility that these recovered "memories" resulted from Farro's imposition of her unitary theory on her client's psyche, not from Heyward's history (p. 92). In order to consider this possibility, which in fact turned out to be the case, the psychiatrist would have had to deconstruct both sides of the contradiction. She would have had to realize that reality is a relational construction, that no one view is primary or universally true, and that what goes on inside a person is an ongoing effect of the particular relations in which he or she is participating. In other words, she would have had to take seriously Heyward's different knowledge that her suffering in the therapy was an effect of her relation with the psychiatrist.

A second contradiction lies at the heart of condescension, especially in its therapeutic manifestations. According to almost all of the psychological and theological theorists cited by condescending professionals, desire and need motivate all human activities and relations. The attempt to deny desire and need intensifies them. Suppressed desire and need express themselves in distorted and often highly destructive forms in the activity or relation in which they are denied. Yet, these professionals, including some of the theorists cited, construct a professional ethic requiring that professionals altruistically renounce their own desires and needs in relation to clients.[24] Alice Miller, one of the psychological theorists most often cited by condescending professionals, traces the origins of altruism to the narcissistic desire to maintain a certain image of the self.[25] Heyward describes the predictable effects of the altruistic therapeutic ethic. As Farro sought to rule out the possibility and the reality of a mutually desiring and needing relationship with her client, the psychiatrist became more, not less (as the altruistic ethic wrongly predicts), angry and passionate with Heyward. In the face of this loss of control, she showed all the signs of an overwhelming need to maintain a certain image of herself as in control. If, as a client, Farro had described her feelings and activities to a therapist like herself, her therapist would have had no difficulty pointing out the contradiction between her attempted renunciation and the resulting intensification of her desires. Heyward demonstrates that the condescending attempt to purify professional power of desire and need inevitably results in the intensification of desire and need. A therapist caught in the contradiction between renunciation and overwhelming needs and desires can easily abuse the client whose presence seems to ignite the conflict. Farro blamed and punished Heyward for the contradiction that she, the psychiatrist, had brought into the therapy.

In Heyward's telling, both she and Farro constructed the

injuring therapeutic relation. They also constructed each other. Heyward's recovered "memories" originated in the psychiatrist's theories and fantasies. They were evidence of the existence of Farro as an internal player in Heyward's psyche. At the same time as she produced these "memories," Heyward was enacting a drama in Farro's psyche; the psychiatrist had incorporated Heyward into herself.

Condescending professionals diagnose such a loss of boundaries as itself pathological and unethical. For example, Heyward's critics claim that whatever went wrong in Farro's therapy with Heyward stemmed from the erosion of the boundaries between the two. They attack Heyward because she does not agree with them. They commend Farro for attempting to establish clear boundaries between herself and Heyward.

Heyward's account undermines the condescending professional diagnosis in three ways. Her close description of the course of therapy reveals what experienced therapist and clients (though, apparently, not Heyward's critics) know, just how fluid, porous, and transitory the boundaries between the therapist and client become during the course of therapy. Some therapists, though not her critics, accept Heyward's second observation, that healing stems from this intimacy in which boundaries become translucent and sometimes disappear. In other words, healing emerges from that reality Heyward's professional critics consider to be pathological and unethical. A few prominent therapists, though again emphatically not Heyward's critics, affirm Heyward's incisive insights about why and how therapy goes wrong. Heyward's account shows that therapy afflicts clients not, as her critics claim, when the boundaries between therapists and clients break down, but when therapists react to this inevitable erosion by attempting to erect clear and rigid boundaries and when clients acquiesce in this futile work to construct an illusion. In other words, Heyward shows that therapeutic actions her critics define as ethical in fact afflict clients.

Recognition of Heyward's and the psychiatrist's co-creativity does not absolve Farro from primary responsibility for Heyward's suffering. The psychiatrist initiated the emotional injury when she, albeit unintentionally, denied both Heyward's knowledge and her ability to act in the therapy. Farro exacerbated the suffering when she rejected Heyward's attempts to end the therapy and to heal the relation through an honest discussion of what had happened between them.

A world in which those who have been oppressed become co-creative subjects is necessarily plural. Different agents in different social locations with different perceptions construct it. A static, single, unified, centralized agent, theory, narrative, or image does not and cannot accurately represent this world. A master subject with a master conception, no matter how critical of established power, finally serves an oppressive and dominating elite by denying the legitimacy and even the existence of plural agents, divergent conceptions, and the different ways of living from which these alternative constructions grow. Liberation is from a world organized around a single ruling agent into reality as a relational web with plural agents and plural ways of conceiving and living. In Heyward's case, healing occurred in such a plural womb. Friends, a lover, other AA members, colleagues, therapists, and the internal manifestations of her father and the divine Sophie all joined their different and divergent voices to Heyward's; together, they constructed Heyward's healing.

The struggle between dominant elites and revolutionary classes is not only over which ethical norm is primary—for instance, condescension or mutuality—and between different worlds—for instance, the world organized around a single center and the world as a web of related centers; it is also over the movements between experience, theory, and action. Privileged elites maintain their domination through the imposition of unifying ideologies or theories that negate subjugated peoples' experiences. Each new revolutionary class must assert the authority of its own divergent experiences over against these negations. Such liberating assertions shatter the unifying conceptions. Entrenched elites respond to such eruptions with renewed negations of the subjugated group's experiences and with reassertions of the dominating ideologies. In other words, dominating elites begin with a theory. They use this theory to negate and appropriate the divergent experiences, emergent theories, and disruptive activities of revolutionary groups. Revolutionary groups, on the other hand, begin, return to, and end with their divergent experiences. Theories are the means by which these subversive groups articulate, claim, and assert the authority of these experiences. Because dominant elites quickly incorporate such disruptive theories into ruling ideologies, revolutionary classes must repeatedly return to the ground of their experiences in order to reform their theoretical weapons. For dominant elites, experience conforms to and action maintains a dominant, unifying theory. For emergent revolutionary groups, provisional and continually revised theories articulate subjugated experiences and so serve as tools of liberation.

Heyward's professional and academic critics counter her revolutionary work with both direct and indirect negations. They deny Heyward's experiences of oppression. They distort what she writes. They repeatedly imply or state that she sought an overtly sexual relation with Farro.[26] In the book, Heyward explicitly differentiates between an erotic friendship and sex (pp. 47, 51, 67-69). For her, any true friendship is erotic, born of mutual desire. Heyward explicitly states that she sought friendship, not a sexual relationship, with Farro (pp. 47, 51). And, again, contrary to her critics' implications, she did not seek such a friendship outside of the therapeutic relation while it continued.

These critics cannot deny Heyward's disruptive passion. And

so, beginning with Farro, they attempt to appropriate it into their existing theories. They do so by using the currently ubiquitous tactic of interpretation. Negating Heyward's own articulation of her experiences, they find in Heyward's account a hidden logic that confirms their unifying ideology. Farro interpreted Heyward's suffering as caused by severe childhood abuse. Most of Heyward's critical reviewers deploy interpretation only as a secondary tactic, relying primarily on direct negation. They toss off a comment that Heyward was involved in an intense transference[27] or express condescending concern about how much the therapy injured her, implying that her own pathology causes her hurt.[28]

Of these critics, only K. Roberts Skerrett deploys interpretation as a primary tactic. She (I am guessing that Skerrett is a woman) seeks to show that "a conventional erotic complaint" hides in Heyward's account. She sifts the text for clues and finds the story she is looking for. She thus accomplishes the task of reducing *When Boundaries Betray Us* to a common love story that confirms rather than subverts patriarchal power.[29]

Her seemingly careful reading makes her presentation far more convincing than those of the other critical reviewers, whose wild negations sometimes leave me wondering if they have actually read the book. Only a close comparison of Skerrett's review and the book reveals just how selective and distorting this interpretation is.

What is most significant, Skerrett dismisses the crucial fact that the relation between Heyward and Farro was a therapeutic one.[30] This negation allows her to abstract Heyward's experiences out of their particular political and social context and to interpret them, not as those of a client, but as those of a generic person in relation to another generic person. A second dismissal, of Heyward's differentiation between an erotic friendship and a genital sexual relation, allows her to interpret Heyward as Farro's would-be suitor.[31]

Having constructed, through interpretation, this common-place situation, Skerrett reduces Heyward's account to the story of a persistent lover who is unwilling to accept a repeated "no" from the object of her passion.[32] Skerrett ends by portraying Heyward as violating the victim Farro.[33] Skerrett thus uses interpretation not only to negate the specificity of Heyward's experiences as a client, but to turn her account on its head. The afflicted one becomes the one who afflicts.

Skerrett sets up this attack at the beginning of her review when she interprets Heyward's actions as an intentional attempt to put a particular feminist theory into action.[34] In so doing, she constructs Heyward as her mirror. For it is Skerrett, not Heyward, who begins her text with a theory, puts this theory into practice by using it to interpret Heyward's book and experiences, and then confirms her theory by comparing it to what she has constructed.

Skerrett demonstrates the oppressive uses of interpretation. Privileged elites deploy interpretation to dismantle revolutionary articulations of subjugated and divergent experiences and to construct in their place abstract and generic stories that confirm the ideologies of domination.

In actuality, Heyward is not Skerrett's mirror. Heyward's revolutionary activity is not an enactment of a theory, but flows from her commitment to her own and others' liberation. This commitment grounds itself in the specificity of her experiences of suffering—in this book, of her oppression as a client. She immerses herself in the particularity of these experiences in order to trace the causes of her suffering and to find ways of liberating herself and others from oppression. She discovers the sources of her affliction in the professional ethic of rigid boundaries that Farro espoused. She repeatedly attempted to engage Farro, even after the psychiatrist's repeated rejections of her, not out of some ethically misguided and abusive infatuation or transference, but out of her realization that her affliction was relationally constructed. Full healing from oppression does not happen without the participation of all those involved. Fully liberating healing only happens when afflicted individuals confront the particular others who have injured them and when those who afflict face, confess, and renounce their participation in oppression of those they have injured. Full liberation requires the healing of the specific relations to the particular and different others through which we constitute each other and our shared realities.

Tragedies are not, as Skerrett asserts, the inevitable effects of an abstract and universal tension between the self and others.[35] Like abuse and healing, oppression and liberation, tragedies arise out of particular meetings. The break between Heyward and Farro is tragic precisely because it is not inevitable. It is a specific tear in the fabric of a relation that shaped and continues to shape both of them. This rent continues to oppress Heyward and probably also Farro. One cannot grasp this tragedy without confronting its specificity, without taking seriously the fact that Farro was Heyward's therapist, without respecting Heyward's differentiations between friendship and sex, and without immersing oneself in the sometimes conflicting and divergent details of the story of this relation.

Heyward begins this book with this immersion in the particularities of her therapy with Farro. She moves from this close examination of experiences to theory and then to practice. The book is a piece of qualitative research in the strictest sense. She begins with particular data and then constructs hypotheses. Two characteristics distinguish this book from most social scientific, literary, historical, and clinical research. Heyward's focus is not primarily on a reality existing apart from herself. The data she explores are her own experiences. And her purpose is not to interpret these experiences, to reduce them to a unitary, theoretical reality. Like Marx, Heyward seeks, through her research, to change reality.[36]

In this focus and commitment, the book is revolutionary. By treating her experiences as a client as the source of insights about how to change an oppressive reality, she redefines clients as authorities. Their knowledge and insights heal and liberate. Liberation comes from the oppressed—in modern industrialized societies, from clients.

The book is a demonstration of the principles of a liberation research methodology. Such research begins from the social location of the oppressed. Especially for someone who is privileged in an advanced industrialized society, this principle requires a shift in consciousness and identity. Heyward instructs the rest of us who are privileged, but who are also committed to liberation, to identify, locate ourselves in, and know reality from our particular places of oppression. From these places, these subjugated identities that exist even in the most privileged people, we learn how oppression works and how to resist it.

Liberation research focuses on the details of what we know from the place of our suffering. It does not rely on preexisting theories or models. The details of our experiences as oppressed are the ground of insights that repeatedly shatter views of the world organized around a single center. Liberation research is a continual cycle of making provisional theories to articulate the insights that emerge from the details of our experiences as oppressed and then returning to the details and so finding new insights that disrupt and change these working theories.

The purpose of liberation research is thus not the construction of a final, unified theory that provides us with a comprehensive interpretation of ourselves and the world. Theory is tool of liberation, of changing reality. A theory is valuable to the extent that it opens up a space in which people and realities heretofore excluded from full participation achieve their power to co-create the world. In her theoretical reflections, Heyward opens up a space in which clients achieve their power to participate in the construction of reality. In her method, she demonstrates how others can open up such spaces.

In summary, this book is "an act of liberation" that Heyward performs for all clients, which means all of us.[37] As one who needs and desires such liberation, I rejoice in it. It gives me strength for the struggle.

Preface (1999)

Carter Heyward

When Boundaries Betray Us was first published in 1993. It was the culmination of a five-year healing process in my life, a process of sorting through the psychospiritual rubble left by a devastating psychotherapy relationship between myself and a therapist to whom I had turned for help in the early years of my recovery from addiction. From its inception, the book was meant to be basically a theological resource for those seeking healing and those providing resources for it. It was meant to lure readers beyond the lines (or "boundaries") that we too easily have drawn between not only "patient" (parishioner, student, client, etc.) and "professional," but also between the aims of personal healing and the opportunities for us all (doctors and patients, priests and laity, teachers and students, etc.) to struggle together on behalf of a more fully just and liberating society and more deeply humanizing and respectful institutions.

I hoped that *When Boundaries Betray Us* might spark a little movement toward this end and, in small pockets here and there, it did. From Ontario, Dublin, Tokyo, Hong Kong, Canberra,

London, Cape Town, and other places around the world and across the United States came messages from patients and clients, counselors and shrinks, religious folk lay and clergy—saying things like, "This has been my experience too.""We need to overhaul the whole system if anyone's ever going to be healed.""I gave your book to my therapist.""I gave your book to my patients.""At last someone speaking for patients!""Thank you for naming the truth." Or, most often, simply "Thank you."

But the loudest public response to the book was anger. *When Boundaries Betray Us* stirred a hornet's nest of professional rage and condemnation of the book and of me (as both author and therapy patient—"the patient from hell," one reviewer concluded). Over time, I began to notice something: The rage of many readers (directed against me as author) seemed to mirror the rage of the therapist (directed against me as patient). How difficult it seemed to be, in both contexts, for folks to accept this patient/author/me as simultaneously vulnerable and strong, needy and confident, often confused but basically functional, sometimes strung out but a more or less "together" woman. I suspected that, like my therapist Elizabeth Farro, these readers were furious at me because they didn't trust me. But why didn't they trust me? It was as if, by presenting myself in this book as both hurt and strong, needy and empowering in the same context and moment, I was toying with their best sense of what is in fact possible. Some readers, especially therapists, seemed unable to conceive of a patient being simultaneously very needy and very well. A few armchair critics diagnosed me as a "borderline personality" who was using my power as a professional priest and writer to exact revenge upon my poor therapist.

As a therapy patient, I did not assume that my therapist would see me primarily as a theologian. I had hoped, however, that she would grant some credence and pay some respect to that vital dimension of my life. As an author, I assumed that many readers of

When Boundaries Betray Us, especially other theologians and pastoral caregivers, would read me primarily as a theologian, because the work that I do—whether about boundaries or Nicaragua, sexuality or Jesus, and whether as patient, teacher, or simply as earthcreature—is always theological. By that I mean it is simultaneously spiritual and political, always seeking connections, always interested in power relations, always interested in struggling for justice. I am never outside the theological arena. I do not aspire to be and I do not intend to be. This was true in my therapy, just as it is in my teaching, writing, dog-walking, cooking, photography, lovemaking, and protesting injustice.

Perhaps I failed to make clear in the text itself that *When Boundaries Betray Us* is a theological book, not merely a personal story or a psychological study. But perhaps it is for you, the reader (much as it was for my therapist) to decide this. Certainly you will have your own responses to the questions raised here about power and healing, friendship and mutuality, and how we go about building this world together, questions that are to me thoroughly theological. However you interpret this book, I hope you will find this reading a provocative, challenging, and creative endeavor.

Special thanks to those friends and colleague who worked with me through the healing processes recounted in these pages—especially Jan Surrey, Demaris Wehr, Miriam Greenspan, Susan DeMattos, Peggy Hanley-Hackenbruck, Jim Lassen-Willems, Sister Angela, c.c., Jeri Kelsey, Margo Rivera, Ann Heyward, Robbie Heyward, and my long-term companion Beverly Harrison. Great appreciation also to Roy SteinhoffSmith for his fascinating and insightful Foreword to this 1999 edition; to Kandace Hawkinson, who edited the 1993 publication for Harper San Francisco; to Timothy Staveteig for encouraging me to republish with Pilgrim Press and taking it under his editorial wing; and to Ed Huddleston at Pilgrim for his work on this project.

Introduction

THIS IS A STORY about a psychotherapy relationship. It is a story of woundedness, healing, and liberation. A story about white middle-strata lesbian women's lives.[1] About addiction and recovery. About professional rules that have come to be called "ethics." It is a story of fear and boundaries and loss and grief. It is also a story of discovery and empowerment. It is more than anything a story about spiritual movement through the transformative power of friendship and, as such, is an invitation into radical social and personal change.

My purpose in these pages is to help sharpen awareness among healers and those seeking healing and liberation that an immutable "power-over" dynamic that does not move us toward a more shared connection serves to diminish and mute the human spirit—even in well-intended, carefully structured professional situations such as psychotherapy.

The story on which this book is based has its own tenderness and, in a very small and particular way, tragedy. But it is a larger picture—the elusive, purposely invisible social backdrop to the personal story—that invites serious reflection. The dynamics between "Dr. Elizabeth Farro" (the pseudonym I have chosen for my former psychotherapist) and me provide, I trust, some critical insight into the painful complexities and consequences of a professional relationship that becomes itself a window into the structures of what we have come to accept as normal power-relations in white western patriarchy.

For eighteen months in 1987–88, Elizabeth Farro and I met regularly, usually once or twice a week (during summers, once a month for a larger block of time: four hours over a two-day period). While we were not sexual lovers, our relationship became increasingly embroiled in dynamics that confounded us both and, in my case, my closest friends as well.

Many contemporary psychological observers would say that Elizabeth and I had a "boundary" problem. We most certainly did, but not in the sense that most therapists would mean. My experience of what happened between us—the account recorded in this book—does not support the prevailing assumption among psychotherapists that they must maintain their "professional boundaries" in order not to harm those who seek their help. Much to the contrary, I experienced Elizabeth Farro's participation in my healing to be strongest and clearest in those moments when she engaged me most fully as a *sister*, most authentically as *herself*, rather than as tightly constricted by a sense of professional correctness. As a theologian, I would say that the power for healing in the therapy, a *sacred* power, was most effective whenever

Elizabeth and I were experiencing it most fully as *ours,* not simply as hers or mine.

This book bears witness to our struggle, Elizabeth Farro's and mine, to celebrate the sacred power we were tapping together. We did not succeed, and, in these pages, I attempt with friends and colleagues to explore why.

I hope the reader will bear with the telling of the particular story, not allowing herself or himself to be seduced into pathologizing either Elizabeth Farro or me. To do so would be to miss entirely the point of this book, which is that the roots of both our personal wounds and our power for healing go far beyond any of our lives as individual selves with separate stories.

On reading an earlier draft of this manuscript, a young friend wrote that she read it as a story of "what happens to passionate little girls." It is indeed a book about what happens to passionate, free-spirited *people* in our society—especially little girls and later adult women. Of course little boys and grown men suffer a similar squelching of the Spirit. But, perhaps because they are men in patriarchy, and especially if they are white men with ample economic privilege, they often are better defended than many women and many men of color against the devastating sense of loss that accompanies the battering of the soul—the "place" in which is seeded our passion for life and love, our yearning for connection and for justice and for the possibilities of creating something new.

The book reflects the need of many women to *have* big sisters and *be* big sisters in a social order in which the bonds of a strong sisterly love seldom are taken seriously as a resource for healing or liberation. These pages tell of an erotically empowering love between women and of our fear of this love, a fear historically well cultivated among us.[2] The book documents a fierce spiritual reckoning between the father-god of christianity and the sacred healing power of mutual relation.

From a more analytically philosophical perspective, the book is about a difficult personal passage beyond the psychospiritual violence set in place by patriarchal logic. This may sound like a technical philosophical term—*patriarchal logic*—but that is not my intention. I use the term from time to time in these pages as a kind of shorthand for the ways in which our lives are organized, ways we for the most part take for granted and do not even notice—ways in which our psyches, spiritualities, work, relationships, and cultural and professional traditions are organized. The whole of our lives and our life together functions to hold in place the economic and social power of privileged white men.

In this book, patriarchal logic refers to the systemic, pervasive ordering of our bodies/minds/souls/selves in relation to one another through a hierarchical construction of unchanging power-relations. In this manmade world, certain people—"the fathers"—are ordained by birth, race, class, religion, education, profession, custom, accumulation of wealth, or simply by their gendered genital structure, to hold and use power over others in a way that is benign, ethical, "logical": that is, both to "help others" and to secure their own power so that it does not change hands; thus, power—the actual embodied ability to effect change, to make things happen, to create—is, by definition, *patriarchal* power, passed on from generation to generation.

The logic of patriarchal power-relations shapes how we reason and how we feel and think about ourselves, one another, and the world. It determines how we draw conclusions, how we draw pictures, how we paint and sing. It keeps us from going outside the lines and from making musical noises that are unfamiliar to us. Patriarchal logic shapes our values, our theologies and ethics. It determines the boundaries within which we are permitted to act, change, or even imagine what may be possible. By *we* and *us*, I mean human beings born and socialized anywhere in the world of patriarchal power-relations, but especially in the context I know best: this white-dominated, male-defined, profit-driven militaristic society organized to maintain and increase the power of those who historically have been white, economically privileged, ostensibly heterosexual males. These pages attempt to shed some light on the devastating relational effects of patriarchal logic.

MEMORY AS RECONSTRUCTION: THE BASIS OF THIS BOOK

Memory is socially constructed. We literally shape our own memories: we do not remember "the Truth" but rather only what part of the truth we can bear to remember; what we can recall; what we are "ready" to see, hear, feel, and think about again. We remember whatever of our past we can, and we do not remember what we cannot. As survivors of childhood sexual abuse are demonstrating, we often do not remember what actually has happened in our lives until conditions in our social world, such as the presence of supportive people, enable us to reach back—emotionally, mentally, physically, and spiritually—toward knowing that something happened and, gradually, toward knowing what it was. Even then, we know only what *we* remember unless others who, in some way, shared our experiences remember it *with* us, in which case we have a more complete understanding of the truth of what happened in a particular moment of our lives.

This book is based almost entirely on *my reconstruction* of what happened in my relationship with Elizabeth Farro and of what transpired over the next several years as my companions helped me begin to heal from the wounding in therapy. In order to "check" my memory, I asked all the characters in this book to read the parts pertaining to them and to tell me if, and how, I might more fully represent the truth of what transpired between us in each case. All of the conversations in the book, except those between Elizabeth and me, reflect this collaborative dimension in their reconstruction.

But what of Elizabeth and me and the transparently one-sided presentation of what took place between us? Simply this: the book would be more completely true and, perhaps, even a very wonderful book if Elizabeth and I had written it together. It would also be an entirely different book. As it is, I have no way to present "the whole truth." I have tried to present as much truth as possible, trusting that this partial truth is both incomplete and honest. It is, I suppose, fair and true to suggest that Elizabeth's silence is her truth in relation to me and that, like mine, her truth is partial, incomplete, and as honest a truth as she can offer.

One other important caveat on the interpretation of Elizabeth: although I have tried to reconstruct the relationship honestly in every way that has seemed to me significant to what transpired between us, I have also purposely constructed Dr. Elizabeth Farro's character in such a way as to protect the identity of the real person.

This is also true of several other characters in the book who asked that I attempt to conceal their identities. The voices of *every* character in the book, those with pseudonyms and those whose real names appear, have been filtered through my perceptions, and although everyone has been able to revise my presentation of their words, it remains true that every character's voice has been constructed through my memory and, in that sense, reflects what I have been able to hear. This admission does not, I trust, dilute the truths in these pages but rather clarifies the radically subjective basis of my presentations of truths, which are honest, partial, and mine. You the readers, like many characters I have cited, can say whether these partial truths are also yours.

Memory is a primary theme, as well as method, in this book. Part of the story is my memory of experiences that were *not*, in autobiographical fact, my own. I make this admission, and hope it will be heard, in a spirit of profound respect for those countless women and men who are remembering having been abused as children. A willingness to believe, or at least to suspend disbelief, is especially important in the context of a patriarchally structured society, in which large numbers of professionals are tending to trivialize or dismiss women's (and some men's) memories of incidents of sexual abuse in their childhoods. There even has arisen in the last few years or so an association of mental-health professionals who are interested in what they call a "false memory syndrome." I don't know enough about FMS to have a well-informed opinion of what truths may be embedded in this new perception, and I imagine there are some, but I suspect that the false-memory-syndrome people are colluding—unawares, I would hope—with significant numbers of sexually abusive persons who don't want to be discovered: parents, for example, who have a vested interest in making it appear that their child has had a false memory of incest. In this book I wish to stand, insofar as I can, with those who have been violated, sexually or otherwise, by parents, siblings, neighbors, clergy, teachers, therapists, spouses, children (in relation to elderly parents), and others. I do not believe that the majority of persons who remember abuse are having false memories.

At the same time, I am clear, through my own experience, that remembering is no simple process and that memory may lead us beyond our individual selves into the experiences of others. Therapists, counselors, clients, and other persons involved in healing need to learn to hold this possibility before us in our work, writing off neither the likelihood that some actual autobiographical experiences often are being remembered nor the possibility that something "other" is being tapped. We can perhaps remember *through* one another's lives—remember *truly* what has happened, but not to us. It seems to me that the last thing we need in this context—whether we are healers or those seeking healing in the moment—is to be burdened with yet another psychological category ("false memory syndrome") that is likely to make those with memories and those working with them experience all the more shame, guilt, and confusion.

We should not dismiss anyone's pain or memory, regardless of what the memory may be pointing to. Rather, we should be working together to learn how to take seriously possibilities we cannot fathom on our own or dare to imagine. Surely this is a good example of why healers and those who seek healing need also to be working together in ways and arenas that are large enough to contain whatever may be happening between us in the mysterious realms of memory and relational power.

ETHICAL ISSUES IN WRITING AND PUBLISHING THIS BOOK

The book has taken almost three years to finish. It has been the most challenging, difficult writing project in my life, for two reasons. First, it has been an immensely painful endeavor emotionally, which I think is clear in its pages. The further along I've moved—both in time, from the therapeutic relationship, and with the manuscript— the more deeply I have come to understand the meanings of the story, the reasons for the pain, and why it is important to share what happened. With this understanding have come a lifting of much of the pain and a personal sense of relief.

Second, I have been sorrowful about Elizabeth's silence in this project. In August 1991, I mailed her an earlier, much less formed version of the manuscript, inviting her response and her participation in its shaping. Again, in December 1992, I sent her several sections of the final draft and said that I would interrupt the process of publication if she wished even to consider joining her voice and perspective with others in this book. I would have been willing to revise these pages, or, more likely, reconceive the project entirely, with Elizabeth. These gestures have been in keeping with my occasional efforts, since the termination of therapy in 1988, to open conversation with her about our relationship, possibly with a third party to help us. With the exception of one letter, early in 1989, in which she directed me not to contact her again, Elizabeth's response to me, and to this book, has been silence.

Although her silence, I believe, has been relationally irresponsible (though professionally correct, some would insist), speaking in relation to it has required an empathic effort to feel with the silent sister, to put myself in her place insofar as possible, to allow her silence to speak to me. I have tried to do this. As the pages that follow suggest, I have solicited help toward this end from a number of psychotherapists who have shared with me stories from their own practices and have told me what, they imagine, Elizabeth might have been experiencing in her work with me. A number of these therapists, and other women and men, read the manuscript in its earlier incarnations and provided much critical response for the revision process. I took especially seriously every suggestion I received on how I might be fairer and more just in my presentation of the Elizabeth character.

Throughout this process of writing, until as recently as the fall of 1992, I had some lingering reservations about whether it would be ethical—right—for me to publish the manuscript, given Elizabeth's absence from the project and yet the centrality of her role in it. Through conversation with people whose lives I trust, and through my own uneven capacity to discern right and wrong—a capacity being forever challenged and seasoned in relation to those whose lives I trust—I decided that this book *should* be published, for two reasons:

First, I believe that what I have written is more likely to contribute to the making of right-relation among those who read it than to impede this possibility. That is to say, it is, I think, more likely to help people live and work ethically and compassionately than to hinder them.

Second, I believe that for me, in effect, to join in Elizabeth's silence would be to collude in upholding a professional tradition that often silences the most honest and compassionate voices of both professional healers and those who seek their help, thereby disconnecting us and disallowing a mutual opportunity for healing and liberation. I have come to believe that this silence should be broken as often and carefully as possible by both healers and those who have sought healing. Thus, I have come to believe that the primary ethical warrant for this publication is to help shatter a contemptuous silence that wounds and diminishes the human spirit.

THE PIVOTAL ROLE OF FRIENDSHIP IN THIS BOOK

As these pages will show, my desire to build a friendship with Elizabeth following the termination of therapy became, over time, the driving force in our relationship and led eventually to its painful rupture. It was not then, and is not now, the case that I think therapists "should" become social friends with all their former clients any more than teachers or priests like myself "should" or can become friends with everyone with whom we work. I am, however, challenging as *unethical* any so-called ethic that rules out the cultivation of genuinely mutual relation anywhere in our lives. What a frightful commentary such a rule is on our incapacity to imagine healing the fear-based splits in our lives between work and love, public and private, the power to heal and the power to be-friend.

Conscientious healing professionals today are trying to be genuinely ethical—nonabusive—in our work. It is important that, in this morally critical moment in which abuse, the misuse of power, is flagrant and systemic, those of us who work as healers—therapists, doctors, nurses, priests, pastors, rabbis, educators, midwives—understand how badly abusive we can be by withholding intimacy and authentic emotional connection from those who seek our help. For "abuse" is not simply a matter of touching people wrongly. It is, as basically, a failure to make right-relation, a refusal to touch people rightly. We as professionals—indeed, we as people on this planet—are as likely to destroy one another and ourselves by holding tightly to prescribed role definitions as we are by active intrusion and violation.

mutuality

In relation to Elizabeth, I was yearning for right-relation. In order to trust the healing dynamic at work between us, which I—and, I believe, Elizabeth also—had experienced as a profoundly shared, creative power from the day we met, I needed assurance that this, in fact, was the case; that Elizabeth also was experiencing the dynamic between us as mutually empowering. Otherwise, either I was deluded or she was merely acting a part. In either case, if she was not being touched and changed with me, I could not experience the relationship as trustworthy. I believe strongly that we are genuinely healed, strengthened, and liberated *only* insofar as our relational energy is calling us both, or all, to life, to be who we are at our best together. Unless the healer is being transformed by the therapy process and the teacher being changed with her students, these relationships are not trustworthy resources for authentic spiritual growth or emotional well-being.

In this context, the possibility of a future friendship became for me a sign of Elizabeth's openness to honoring a connection we already had begun to forge. As a friend someday, Elizabeth could let me know how our relationship had been changing her, what she had experienced during my therapy, how she really felt about me, what she had been given through our work together, what difference my passion and questions and struggles and celebrations had made to her, and what she, as a sister, had been discovering with me about herself and the world. Friendship meant that we would attempt to stay connected beyond psychotherapy in ways that honored us both and respected both of our lives.

I slowly would come to realize that my longing for the ongoingness of this relationship was wonderfully healthy and right, despite assumptions of traditional psychological systems that tend to value autonomy and separation over connection and interdependence as goals in psychotherapy. My yearning to stay connected reflected my faith in the power of mutual relation that I had experienced with Elizabeth, the sacred energy we had been tapping together, the spirited force that already had touched and was beginning to transform our lives—*both* of our lives, I trusted. Perhaps, as friends further down the road, Elizabeth and I would have enjoyed seeing each other occasionally at professional meetings and talking together. More likely, we also would have become sisterly companions, seeking to cultivate the learnings and joy we had begun to share. This was what friendship meant to me in relation to Elizabeth.

The saddest and, to me, most troubling aspect of what transpired between us is that, with the weight of the traditional psychiatric profession behind her, Elizabeth chose to disengage entirely from me rather than struggle with me toward a less final and wounding solution. There is a serious distortion in any ethic, professional or other, that breaks connection, sending people into separate illusions of "safe space." The fact is that this break did not leave me "safe" in any way, and I suspect something similar was true for Elizabeth. I imagine we both had to begin, separately, with whatever resources we could find, to deal with the damage that had been done, and the danger we were in.

Over the next several years, I literally was saved through the power of friendship. Without my human and animal friends, I could not have survived the pain of the rupture I had experienced as so terribly wounding. I was left feeling as if I were going mad, which had always been my worst fear. The therapy relationship and its ending had drawn me more deeply than I had ever been into this embodied fear, in which I was unable to trust my own experience of what had been happening to me, in me, with me, or in my presence. This was a recapitulation of my past—a wrenching terror brought on in particular moments when my most soulful passion had been shattered by silence, pathologizing, or rejection. This was how I had experienced Elizabeth's treatment.

But as Elizabeth stepped out, many good friends stepped in and, I am clear, helped not only save my life but also carry me forever beyond my fear of madness. For, if there is one primary lesson in this book—one gift through the healing—it is a deep psychospiritual and political realization that we are born into the world to live passionately together as sister and brother earthcreatures; in that sense, as friends. And no system of doctrine, discipline, ethics, or professional treatment can make it otherwise.

This publication and the experience it represents are in some tension with the perspective of many feminist therapists, counselors, and clergy who, in reaction to the pervasiveness of systemic violence among us, seem to me awash in a language of "professionalism," "boundaries," and "safety." I believe that this language, and the fear beneath it, have become excessive and are strangling our capacities to be genuinely moral with one another. That is, we are becoming rule-bound rather than ethical, obedient rather than struggling honestly together toward creating relational ethics that do not inhibit intimacy. In these dangerous times, it is essential that we find better ways to work and love as moral persons. This is a primary reason I have written, and am sharing, this book.

THE ROLE OF "PRIVILEGE" IN THIS BOOK

Psychotherapy is a class privilege. It is not available to, nor is it desired by, everyone. And there is nothing wrong with women being paid to "hear each other to speech"—to be present relationally, listening, receiving, and responding in such a way that the other is able to find her voice and speak honestly.[3] Most of us need to make a living, and we all need help. I do not believe that, as a privilege, psychotherapy is inherently unethical, wrong. But something *is* wrong—ethically, psychologically, spiritually, and politically—when therapists or other helpers approach pain as if it could be treated more or less independently of the social forces, including the privilege, that often have created it and always have helped hold it in place.

Had Elizabeth and I been consciously studying this privilege, we might be friends today. That is, if we had been working together to feel, name, and make connections between my pain and such forces as hetero/sexism and homophobia; class injury and economic exploitation; white privilege and racism; misogyny, sexual violence, and other social forces that have shaped my life, hers, and the psychotherapeutic relationship, I do not believe our relationship would have ruptured. For what shattered our relationship was not only the disconnections of our lives, but our failure to explore these disconnections together, our failure to probe together our fragmentation into pieces that are political *or* spiritual, professional *or* personal, public *or* private, self *or* other, client *or* therapist. What tore us apart is that, despite my deepest yearnings and, I believe, Elizabeth's as well, we were unable to sustain the strong sisterly connection that originally had moved us into a shared sense of joy and excitement at the connections we were beginning to make together about life, the world, and our lives as lesbian women.

And so, we two white middle-strata women sat there for eighteen months, knowing in our souls, I believe, that we were sisters, and becoming increasingly restless together with traditional psychotherapy's foundations of disconnection, in which private and public, professional and personal, therapist and client are never really allowed to meet. We were, for a while, becoming critical together of these splits and this power to damage us both. We were resisting the disconnections, challenging the fragmentation, making connections.

 But social privilege is a seductive emotional master that teaches us to fear connection, awareness, and authentic knowledge of ourselves and one another. And so the same privilege that had brought us into a relationship in which a sisterly bond was being forged by our making connections wound up tearing us apart. Indeed, it was our privilege as professional, middle-strata, white women, a privilege that breeds fear of change and risk, that won the day, for it is precisely this "privilege" that allows us *not* to make connections. *Not* to see what is what. *Not* to see who we really are. Ironically, then, as has been the case with many professional women in this culture, Elizabeth's and my capacity to act like the sisters we are was sacrificed to our "privilege."

REMEMBERING SOPHIE: THE SPIRITUAL STRUGGLE IN THIS BOOK

Several months before my fortieth birthday in 1985, I found a lump in my left breast. It was benign, but the days and nights of unknowing gave me a fresh, intimate glimpse into the reality of the dying that we do. I saw that this dying and living is a constant, inescapably personal movement not only out of life as we know it, but also into other dimensions of it. I began to imagine that every day, one day at a time, we can explore a few of these many dimensions, if we dare. I suspect this had something to do with my decision later in 1985 to stop drinking and, still later, with the related cessation of my compulsive overeating and vomiting. The early period of this healing process opened a floodgate of strong feeling that has become a resource of spiritual transformation.

Because this depth of feeling pulled me into a reckoning with what I most strongly do, and do not, believe, it sparked me also into burnout, emotional exhaustion, in which for a while all I had energy for was sighing and crying—about my father's death; my aging dog, Teraph; the confusing contradictions in being a lesbian christian priest; the callous injustices of the Reagan phenomenon; the devastating toll of AIDS; violence against people of color, Jews, Palestinians, children, women, gaymen, and lesbians. More than anything, this became for me a time of reckoning with God, which I had come to believe over the years is our sacred power in mutual relation.

As a lesbian feminist christian priest, I'd been experiencing what women are shaped to experience by heterosexist patriarchy: abusive social relations in which, to the extent that we envision and try to embody a different way—a nonhierarchical, noncontrolling way of sharing power-with-one-another—we are punished as deviant, trivialized as unrealistic, dismissed as ignorant, or cast out as dangerous. The primary abuse in my life had been *church abuse*, but I was not yet clear just how fully this was so. I needed a helper, a sister-sojourner with me at the core of what it means to be a deviant woman; studying with me these dynamics of abuse; sharing with me the essence of healing, which I had come to believe passionately is the struggle for right, mutually empowering relation. It is a way of being in relation that the church does *not* teach.

On several other occasions during the last couple of decades, I'd gone into therapy to help clarify my commitments and feelings. I'd found these professional relationships useful, and each had remained open beyond therapy to the development of whatever collegial collaboration or friendship might follow. In the winter of 1987, I decided to begin therapy again.

To me, the primary significance of my therapy and its aftermath is the spiritual movement it carried. I am, after all, a daughter of patriarchal logic—born, raised, educated, and expected to be strong and capable but, like Antigone, on the often unspoken but always unmistakable terms set by ruling-class men. I had pretty much lived my life on these terms until, with ten sisters, I was ordained "irregularly" as an Episcopal priest in 1974, before the church had authorized the ordination of women. The irregular ordination was, for me, a turning point. I could not revert spiritually. If I were to keep good faith in the Spirit that had led my sisters and me, and many others with us, to defy the authority of the church, I could not function, beyond this point, as an obedient daughter of church fathers or of the father/god they make and worship in their own image.

Thus, for almost twenty years now, sometimes with joy and delight, sometimes in rage or sadness, along with other women and men of different colors and cultures in patriarchal religion, I have struggled to keep my balance on a very narrow wire. It is a thin cord that separates our acquiescence to the fathers' terms—that is, our participation in hetero/sexist, racist, and/or class-elitist customs, doctrines, discipline, and worship—and a wholesale rejection of patriarchial religious tradition, including its cultures and communities.

I had experienced coming out in 1979 as a lesbian christian priest as such a balancing act. Over the last decade, I'd tried not to lean too far in either direction so as not to fall away from either my christian or my lesbian, gay, and feminist communities, all people with cultures and languages I share, some of them overlapping. I had been working gladly "on the wire," able for the most part to keep a steady balance or to pick myself up whenever I slipped. I had been heartened by the company of others with me and, with them, had been troubled and fascinated by the challenges that met us as both religious and secular institutions of our lives were constricted increasingly during the 1980s by reactionary social, economic, and political forces.

By 1987, however, my time on the wire was up. I was exhausted, yet deeply afraid of the alternatives. Previously, I'd been able to numb out this fear with alcohol and food, but this was no longer the case. I'd been sober and eating more gently for a year and a half. What would happen if I stepped off the wire? What would happen if I stopped trying to balance my love of the church with my love of strong, feisty women who love their sisters, their brothers, and themselves? What would happen if I never again worried about whether I was, am, or will be too pushy, too passionate, and too much myself to be a good christian woman?

Beginning therapy with Elizabeth, I was unaware that the time had come—I was ready—to wrestle seriously with such questions. What indeed *would* happen if I passed through my fear of loss, rejection, and change and simply (or not so simply) let go? This question and its answers would become clearer to me within several months as I began to remember "Sophie," my earliest experience of sacred power, my first image of God. Sophie had been my wise little imaginary playmate when I was a child, and having grown with me (though I seldom had recognized her, I was moving so fast), she would meet me again now, in her adulthood and my own, as Sophia, ancient figure in Jewish and christian literature, image of the Wisdom of God.[4] Remembering Sophie, I would be met by Sophia.

She awaited me, and Elizabeth with me.

Five months into therapy, I would write in my journal:

Sophia is our wisdom, wellspring of all that is true and worth knowing. She comes as Womanpower though She is not a woman nor a gender nor a person at all. She is a transpersonal yearning, a relational motion, a way of being in touch with whatever is most fully creaturely, most radically and passionately ours.

Ruling-class men have feared and suppressed Sophia as a sensual and intelligent image of the divine. They have denied the divine Sophia in the name of the god they have created to keep her in check. Thus, Sophia often can be recognized as a spiritual movement, or dynamic, that generates great fear among us because she urges us to dissent from patriarchal power-relations.

Sophia comes as an irrepressible movement among women and men for justice. She plays with us, lusty lover of strong and lovely women, and sees better than most of us that all women can be strong and lovely. All can be, though it is difficult for any of us to be in these times in which women are pitted against women. It is still hard for us to be sisters to one another or to care very well for ourselves. But Sophia is the constant and friendly resource of this possibility.

For those of us educated in patriarchal, androcentric religious cultures, Sophia's coming catches us off guard. She meets us when we least expect to be touched, much less shaken, by the divine. Most of us spend much of our lives running from Sophia, for we have learned to fear the chaos that will be sparked in our lives when she meets us. We are frightened, for as we see ourselves and one another through her eyes, we see the possibility of living more simply and honestly as sisters, brothers, and friends. Gaining our freedom, we pass through our fear.

THE SHAPE AND TITLE OF THIS BOOK

Throughout the book are poem-prayers to Sophie/Sophia from the journal I have kept erratically throughout much of my life and more intentionally for the duration of therapy and the years following its termination. By *journal,* I mean scribblings in margins of essays, notes to myself on the inside covers of books, and writings on notepads, envelopes, gasoline receipts, ticket stubs—anything available when I have needed to write. Over the years, I have occasionally saved these jottings. I kept many of them during and after therapy and have drawn upon them in preparing this manuscript. The journal has contained not only the poem-prayers but also notes I made about therapy, at times in greater detail than at other times. Hence, some of the dialogues with Elizabeth, as presented in this book, are much more nearly verbatim than others that have been reconstructed largely on the basis of my memory and feeling.

Jan Surrey is a sister who has worked intentionally and intimately with me throughout this healing process. I am grateful for her compassionate Afterword (which was the Foreword to the previous edition). Part 1 is the reconstructed story of my therapy with Elizabeth, and in Part 2, several resources (twelve-step recovery, vocational commitments, close friendships, and prayer and meditation) are interwoven to produce five patterns of sacred power that have been healing me—patterns of voice, mutuality, earthcreature, compassion, and ambiguity. Part 3 highlights several of the most critical ongoing issues for me through this experience. Finally, the Selected Readings are included to amplify the volume's theoretical dimensions.

The title emerged gradually and became clear only at the end, literally as the book was headed to press. Like the manuscript, it reflects an intensely collaborative effort among editors, author, and friends. I am especially pleased that "When Boundaries Betray Us" conveys truthfully what this book is about, but also, I imagine, it is a title Elizabeth Farro and I could have chosen together had *we* been writing *our* book rather than simply I writing mine. For I believe not only that I was wronged but that Elizabeth Farro herself and the relationship we had begun to build also were betrayed by what transpired between us.

Finishing this project, I am aware of my lingering sadness at the loss of a sister, a loss that never should have been and should not be. But my heart also sings a serene and grateful song, and this book, I trust, will tell you why.

PART ONE

Wounding
in Therapy

THE WINTER OF 1986–87 was cold and hard for me. Second semester had just begun and I was already exhausted. In truth, I had been exhausted for months, dragging myself from day to day, my intense feelings right beneath the surface. Dr. Elizabeth Farro's name had been given to me by another doctor who didn't know her. She knew only that Dr. Farro was a lesbian. I had taken her name, along with four others, and had begun shopping around for a therapist. She was the second I contacted.

Remembering Sophie

"Dr. Heyward?" Elizabeth asked, responding by phone to my efforts to reach her.

"Yes."

"This is Dr. Elizabeth Farro, returning your call."

"Oh yes, Dr. Farro. Thanks for calling back. I'm considering beginning therapy and my internist has given me your name."

"I see. Can you tell me a little about yourself and what you need?"

"Yes. I'm just plain tired. Exhausted," I sighed. "I'm forty-two, live and work here in Cambridge. I'm a professor of theology at the Episcopal Divinity School. My father died a little over two years ago. A few months later, I had a lump removed from my breast. It was benign, but scary. Then, about a year ago, I stopped drinking, began going to AA, realized that I'm an alcoholic. I'm also bulimic."

"Are you bingeing and purging at this time?"

"No. AA seems to have worked for me there too. I haven't been actively bulimic since I joined AA."

"Anything else?"

"I have an old dog whom I love who'll be dying before long, I'm sure, and that's painful—the thought of letting him go. Oh yes, and I'm also a lesbian, I'm out of the closet, and I'm an Episcopal priest."

"Jesus Christ!" came the response. Dr. Elizabeth Farro sounded like she was ready to leap through the wires to see for herself who or what such a creature must be.

"What a wonderful response," I laughed.

She laughed, too. "No wonder you're tired!"

The exchange was delightful. I wanted to meet her and sensed she felt the same way. We set an appointment for sometime the following week. As I hung up, I laughed out loud and said to myself, "Well, she's not just *any* psychiatrist!"

AT OUR FIRST MEETING, I told her that the sisterly spontaneity and warmth she'd conveyed by phone had drawn me to want to meet her and probably work with her.

"It's also important to me at this time in my life that I work with a lesbian," I said.

"I'm a lesbian," she responded.

I nodded. "Yes, I know."

She raised her brow quizzically.

"Pat Fenner, my internist, told me. That's why I called you."

IT TOOK MAYBE twenty minutes into this meeting for me to know I'd found my helper. There were three clues, as I noted in my journal: I felt at home with her, able to relax, able to plop onto her couch exhausted. I intuited her strong desire to work with me. And I recognized between us the strong, creative presence of the Spirit that moves us into, and toward, mutual relation. I could tell that, with Dr. Elizabeth Farro, I'd be able to receive and give; learn and teach; be moved myself, and move another. I knew we would work *with* each other; that we would grow together, both of us becoming; and that further along we might well become friends.

I hadn't chosen Dr. Farro because she was a psychiatrist, but I was intrigued that she was a *lesbian* psychiatrist. I assumed she would have had experiences not unlike mine as a lesbian priest and that, in our heterosexist, homophobic world, this particular common bond could be a channel for my healing. I also assumed that if the relationship was to be genuinely creative—that is, if it was to be really healing for either of us—it would be so for *both* of us.

For the first couple of sessions, Dr. Elizabeth Farro and I talked about my life and work as a lesbian priest and teacher, and I asked her a little about hers as a lesbian psychiatrist. She told me not very much, but enough for me to feel a sisterly connection between us and to sense that she felt this, too. Already, a week or ten days into therapy, I was beginning to feel my exhaustion lifting. Simply sitting, relaxing, with a sister was sparking the healing power between us.

Two weeks after I began therapy, I traveled to Cornell University. During my sermon in the chapel, a young male student began shouting at me from the balcony at the back of the large Romanesque structure:

"Daughter of Satan! Black bitch! Lesbian witch! Thou shalt not lie with a woman as with a man! Thus saith the Lord! You deserve to die! You will be put to death! . . . " On he went until his colleagues were able to calm him down.

This was not the first time I'd been verbally assaulted, but now, in recovery, I was feeling the violence more intensely than during my drinking years, when I could use alcohol to curb the fear and pain.

I told Elizabeth Farro about this incident. She seemed astonished by it, amazed that I had finished the sermon and mingled with the congregation afterward and dumbfounded to hear that my sister priests, and certainly our gay brothers and lesbian sisters, have grown to expect this in the course of our work.

"How did you feel?" she asked.

"Scared."

"I can imagine!"

"But we go on. We have to. I mean, living involves risking, and dealing with a lot of craziness and fear and hostility. That's what I've learned in the church!" I laughed.

"Well, you could learn it anywhere," she responded.

"Right. How did *you* feel when I told you about this?" I asked her.

"Frightened for you and very sorry this happens to you. I guess it's the price all spiritual and religious leaders pay. I'm very admiring of your willingness to go on. It takes a lot of courage. Not many people have it."

We sat in silence. Then Dr. Elizabeth Farro continued, "How do you prepare for your public presentations? I mean, spiritually, how do you prepare, knowing that this kind of thing might happen?"

"I don't know what you mean by 'prepare.'"

"Do you have a little ritual or quiet time? Is there anything you say or do before you go into the public world?"

"Not really." I was intrigued.

"I'd like to offer you a gift—the gift of knowing that you can always be bathed in white light. You can sit quietly and ask that the light surround you, and protect you, and strengthen you." She spoke slowly and quietly. "You must be very quiet and still in order for this to happen," she continued.

"Yes. I believe you," I said. "It's just been such a long time since I imagined how fully I might be able to experience it." I felt like I was going to cry.

Dr. Elizabeth Farro was looking at me with wide-open and very tender eyes. "You have experienced a lot of pain, haven't you?"

I nodded and felt myself choking back the tears. "I find my work very hard."

"And you do it very well. It's important you take this in and give yourself credit for being a remarkable woman. I don't think you're going to be able to realize this until you learn how to sit quietly with yourself and just be."

I knew that she was speaking the truth. "Yes," I said. "This is what I'm looking for."

"Isn't it called 'serenity' in AA?" she asked.

I nodded.

FOR THE FIRST two months, I met with Elizabeth Farro once a week, to pour my heart out. It was exactly what I needed to do, and it was all that I needed. Not just to speak of pain and tiredness but, as importantly, to give voice to deep, strong, and passionate commitments. For many years I'd needed to take time simply to ask a sister to hear me to speech. To sit with me and be moved spiritually with me into shared realizations of God as our sacred power in mutual relation, the only source available for the healing of broken spirits and the liberation of a broken world.

Dr. Elizabeth Farro was hearing me to speech about the things that matter most to me. And I was beginning to hear myself through the amplifiers of a relationship in which I felt that this sister-healer was being moved with me into a stronger sense of her own relational presence.

I sensed something powerfully mutual between us, and I believed that this something, our power in mutual relation, is our sacred power for healing. I intuited that Elizabeth Farro was seeking a clearer sense of spiritual power in her own life and that she was keenly aware that this power was being generated between us.

"What you say excites me," she responded when I asked how she felt about my experience of erotic power as having as much to do with the Nicaraguan revolution as with genital sexuality, and of my belief that we share a common vocation, she and I and others, to re-create the world on the basis of an ethic of mutual empowerment.

"I want to learn how to *live* this way without burning out," I said. "That's why I'm here. No longer drinking to numb out the pain of failure, disapproval, rejection . . . "

". . . or tiredness," she added. "You're feeling exhausted *be-cause* you're not drinking or bingeing."

"That's interesting," I said. "It makes sense and feels right." It hadn't occurred to me that stopping drinking and compulsive eating would make me feel tired, or would open me up to feeling how tired my body/spirit actually had become over the years. Accumulated exhaustion. Too much church abuse. Not enough mutuality. Not enough affirmation of strong, erotically empowered/empowering women. I had been broken, and badly hurt.

Six weeks into therapy, I was beginning to realize the toll that being an "out" lesbian christian priest had taken. For the first time I began to weep not only for the poor and oppressed whom we readily and publicly can identify as the most brokenhearted and outcast in our world, but also for myself and the many, many sisters who are much like me, sisters like Elizabeth.

We, too, have been brokenhearted and have not known that the pain of the world is ours as well.

I did not see it clearly at the time, but I had found with Dr. Elizabeth Farro a spiritual refuge, a place to take heart in the context of the unspeakable disconnectedness, violence, and denial set in place by patriarchal christianity and culture. I did not know how badly I'd needed a spiritual place to speak boldly and soulfully of the sacred Spirit in whom I'd long believed, and of Her erotic power to touch, comfort, and transform us all in the context of despair and death designed by patriarchal logic. I did not know how badly I'd needed a sacred place and a sister, a soulmate, to sojourn with me in this place. Elizabeth Farro was becoming a soulmate, and I was beginning to love her.

Over the years there had been many women in my life who, in different ways, had mediated the sacred to me. On several occasions—at camp as a teenager, in college, on a retreat during the summer of our irregular ordination—I'd met women older than I who had seemed to me to embody sacred power. They seemed so able, grounded in confidence, clear in their power—big, strong women. In each case, I'd pushed hard at them, wanting somehow to learn from them about women's power, wanting them to lead me to the source of their/our strength.

But white women in western culture usually do not know how to teach girls or other women about our power. Even if we ourselves are empowered in creative, liberating ways, chances are we are not clear about the source of our strength. We are likely to believe it is a gift from a father/god or the result of a well-developed ego, or perhaps even more likely to experience our power as an aberration, a cause for apology, something to be downplayed, a shame. And if we experience our power as erotic, we are most likely terrified of "it," of being ourselves in relation to those women and girls who are drawn to us.

So these women from whom I wanted so badly to learn did not know what to do with an overly enthusiastic teenage dyke, a young adoring woman who needed more than they could give. Again and again, I had been sent away, ashamed of being so needy and, evidently, too demanding.

With Dr. Elizabeth Farro, the situation had seemed to me different—more like my attachment to my high school history teacher, Betty Smith, who had not sent me away but rather had mentored me and later had become a very special friend, which she is to this day; and also like my relationship with Bev Harrison, who once had been my teacher and later had become my best friend in all the world, and my lover. The most striking similarity between Dr. Farro, Bev, and Betty Smith, and that which distinguished them from other women to whom I'd been attached, was that each seemed to be a spiritually searching woman tuned in to a similar openness in me and was, through our relationship, being touched with me.

Through the years and many relationships, my deepest spiritual yearning had been to reconnect with the source of my passion and, in so doing, finally to dispel my fear of being "crazy"—that is, passionate—in a world that treats passionate folks, especially women, as crazy. Only with strong spiritual confidence could I move through my fear of being crazy and learn simply to live.

I had been a christian all my life, a liberation theologian/ activist and priest for almost fifteen years. I needed to sit still and quiet for a while to notice the Spirit that had been with me, and with us all, from the beginning. I had to sit still and quiet with a sister who was opening *with* me to our healing power to become aware in my soul of what I had taught and written for years: that our power is sacred because it is shared.

BUT WHO WAS *Dr. Elizabeth Farro?* Was I simply projecting my yearning onto her? Was I seeing something only in myself and imagining that it belonged to us both? Or was this relationship, as it seemed to me, a window with a sometimes clear, sometimes cloudy view into the very essence of mutuality—the love that it generates and the fear that impedes it?

I experienced Elizabeth Farro as a woman hungry for the movement of the Sacred, longing to be touched and blessed by the Holy, yearning to embody a confidence in this Spirit. I felt this in her face and body, her words and silence. From the outset of our work together, it seemed to me that, through our attentiveness to *my* life and struggle, especially in the church, Elizabeth Farro's and my work together was providing a window for us *both* into the difficulties and ecstasies of living as lesbian women in the Spirit of holiness, justice, and compassion.

Dr. Elizabeth Farro's eyes would sparkle. Her face would become radiant, and there were times when it looked to me as if she were going to levitate. I had spent enough time over the years as a teacher and counselor to spiritually seeking women to intuit when a sister is turned on spiritually, energized, and excited. Elizabeth Farro and I seemed tuned into each other's spiritual sensibilities. Our "antennae" were picking up each other's psychospiritual "waves"; it was exciting to me, and it seemed to be so for her as well.

Often she would seem to come to life during our work. By the end of the session, she would look to me as if she wanted to dance, so filled did she seem with delight and energy.

It is not just the healer who realizes what is happening in therapy. Whenever a genuinely creative moment of relational engagement happens, both (or all) persons are being touched, moved, changed, in the moment—*and both know it.* The client, if she is intuitive and empathic, often knows as much as the therapist about what's going on between them.

"How do you feel right now about what's happening in this room?" I sometimes would ask when the excitement between us seemed to be peaking.

And she would laugh or smile widely, and say, "Great!" or "It's very exciting!" or "Wonderful!"

Throughout the therapy, Dr. Elizabeth Farro's spiritual openness was, I believe, the root of her capacity to treat me well, to meet me as a sister. It was a real and lovely dimension of who this healer was. It was most definitely the basis of my trust.

Is this same spiritual vulnerability—openness to the creative life force—not the core of who we all are at our best: to question, to seek and share, to learn as much as possible about the movement of the Sacred so that, together, we can learn how to be the sisters and brothers we are, vibrant and compassionate in our life on the earth? Is this not the fundamental purpose of life itself, our reason for being, the basis of our capacity to be moral—rightly related—in the context of the violence that threatens to undo us?

In early April, I wrote a short poem, the first of many in the course of my work with Elizabeth Farro. I called it

THERAPY

it never dawned on me
you'd touch not
just my psyche
but my
soul,
nor God knows
that i'd touch
yours.

I didn't give it to her at that time. Several weeks later, however, putting my spirituality into a language I thought she, as a therapist, might find more comprehensible, I told her that I was feeling incredibly drawn to her, as if I were in love with her.

"Now, I know I'm not really 'in love' with you," I was quick to assure, "but I seem to be going through a transference that's quite powerful!"

"Yes, it *is* a transference," Dr. Farro agreed. "This usually happens. It's just happening here much earlier in the therapeutic process than usual, and I'm not sure why." She smiled and was quiet. Then she asked, "What does the transference feel like to you?"

"It feels wonderful, like an incredibly important, creative way of loving from which I can learn a lot about myself, you, our relationship, and life itself." I felt radiant as I spoke. "I've had many students and church people who've experienced intense transference in relation to me. I look upon their experiences and now mine as opportunities for shared growth and learning and, possibly, movement toward friendship."

Elizabeth Farro seemed energized by what I was saying—until I spoke the word *friendship*. At that moment her demeanor shifted abruptly, and for the first time in our work together, she seemed rigid and cold. She sounded to me literally like a different person from the woman I had begun to know. She sounded as if she were reading from a textbook as she spoke to me without affect:

"It is important that I be clear with you and that you understand me. If we had met at a dinner party, we might be friends. Since we met here in this office, we will not be friends. Ours is a professional relationship. Is that clear?"

I remember in that instant not so much my words as my feelings. A pain ripped through my gut, not so much of rejection, but of confusion and contradiction. Who was this person sitting with me, this sister to whom I had been giving so much from my soul? Was this Elizabeth Farro who had just spoken to me? or someone else? Was Dr. Farro, the psychiatrist, a different person?

Was the confusion mine, something in me? Maybe *this* is why I needed therapy. Was Dr. Elizabeth Farro just doing her job? Had I created an illusion that the sharing of passion was, in a real and sacred way, confirming not only my real presence but Elizabeth Farro's as well? Was she a healer who was becoming my sister, or was this a less authentic relational connection than it appeared to be?

I heard the words "we will not be friends." I nodded when she asked if what she had said was clear to me. But in that moment I began to wrestle with the pain I felt and with the confusion and contradictions I had experienced in the dramatic change of personas that took place in Elizabeth Farro right before my eyes. Or had it been only in my mind?

On the way home, I stopped the car long enough to jot my thoughts down on an old gasoline receipt:

"If what she said is true, if a future friendship is ruled out because she is my therapist, then *something is basically untrustworthy about this relationship.*"

From that moment on, this intuition would haunt our relationship.

LATER IN APRIL, in the context of a conversation about the church's treatment of homosexuals, Mary, a sister priest, mentioned to me that a lesbian couple had been to see her to discuss having a ceremony of commitment. She told me very little about them other than that she'd liked them. Later in the conversation, as I was telling Mary about my therapy, it became apparent to her that Elizabeth Farro was one of the two women who'd been to see her, and she told me this. We laughed about the smallness of the world and agreed it would probably be best not to talk further about this, given our shared sense that Dr. Elizabeth Farro would not want such a conversation to be happening.

A week or two later, I told Elizabeth Farro about this. She threw her head back, laughed, then suddenly became very serious and agitated. "How much did she tell you?"

"Not much. We really weren't talking about you and your partner. We were talking about the church."

"She didn't tell you anything about my personal life? I mean, we shared a lot with her and there's a lot she could have told you."

"No. She told me almost nothing."

"Did she tell you *anything?*"

"That your partner's older than you. That she liked you both. That your partner's a professional woman of some sort. That you're a psychiatrist!" I was trying to make light of this, to tease her a bit.

"Well, I don't like this crossing of boundaries. It could be harmful to what we're trying to do here."

"Isn't this a little farfetched?" I asked. "I mean, we're living in the real world, with lives and relationships that overlap. It's not that big a place! Why not just relax and let it be? Don't worry! I respect you and your boundaries."

Dr. Elizabeth Farro looked worried.

ABOUT EIGHT WEEKS into therapy, I began to see her twice a week at my request.

"Why do you want to come twice a week?" she asked.

"Because there's so much going on in me, and now is the right time for me to be doing this work," I responded.

"I agree."

ON APRIL 20, the day of the Boston Marathon, I talked for a while about how athletic and physically strong I'd once been, and we discussed female socialization. This led us into animated conversation about being lesbians in our respective fields, and I left that day feeling strong, good, and connected, as if my exhaustion were finally breaking. In my journal, I wrote: *"How healing it is to sit with a sister who seems to know what I'm talking about. I feel much less lonely."*

"WHAT DO YOU want to be called—Elizabeth or Dr. Farro?" I asked in late April. "I'm tired of not calling you anything."

"What would you like to call me?"

"Elizabeth," I said.

"Why?"

"Because it's more like we're sisters, working *together*, like we're friends. Oh, I know we're *not* friends," I added quickly, "but I have to believe we *could* be."

"And what would it mean for you to call me Dr. Farro?" she asked.

"It would mean, as you've said, that this is, above all, a 'professional relationship.' It would feel very hierarchical and authoritarian, the kind of relationship I'd rather it not be."

"Five years ago, I would not have permitted a patient to call me Elizabeth, but I've changed. You may, if you wish. And what would you like me to call you?"

"As long as I can call you Elizabeth, you're welcome to call me Carter," I responded.

"And if I had asked you to call me Dr. Farro?"

I raised my brow. "I'd ask you to call me Dr. Heyward."

"I see!" She sounded a little surprised. "You have strong feelings about this?"

"Yes."

NOT LONG AFTERWARD, early in May, I went directly to Elizabeth Farro's office from a meeting with Episcopal priests in a neighboring diocese. These clergy had asked me to address them on feminist liberation theology. Speaking in ways that can be heard to christian clergy about power, sex, gender, and structures of race and class privilege as theological issues is arduous mental labor! Arriving in therapy, I was emotionally depleted and discouraged by how defensive *liberal* clergy—men and women—can be about christian tradition, its patriarchal logic notwithstanding. I understand this attitude, having shared it. But in 1987, immersed in spiritual wrestling myself, I was especially sensitive to the psychospiritual violence of christian patriarchy, nowhere more abundant than in gatherings of priests.

Plopping myself onto Elizabeth's sofa, I sat and heaved a huge sigh. "I don't think I can stand any more of this." I shook my head.

"Of what?"

"The church."

We sat silently for a moment.

"You sound very tired," Elizabeth noted.

"I am exhausted!"

"You've just had an exhausting experience?"

I then told her about the meeting, which was, in most significant ways, simply a replication of most professional church meetings and conferences. The story was not new. Neither were the feelings.

Elizabeth pointed this out. "You know you've shared a lot with me about how tired you get in these settings. Do you realize how often you've talked in here about this kind of thing—and we've only been meeting a few weeks!"

I nodded.

"Is this typical of your work in the church? Do you feel beaten up and exhausted when you're with your own professional colleagues?"

Again, I nodded and felt myself begin to well up with tears. Soon I was crying softly, my head buried in my hands. When, after a moment, I glanced at Elizabeth, she met me with a nod that signaled, I trusted, her empathy and solidarity.

"You know," she began, "I've begun to realize, even in the short while we've been working together, how important your work as a theologian is and how many people are leaning on you for support and leadership."

I shook my head. "Not *these* people! They're not looking to me, or leaning on me, for anything. Most of them are terrified of what I represent. . . ."

"Which is?"

"Being a lesbian, feminist, 'irregularly' ordained woman priest, heretic in theology, radical in politics."

"That's what I mean. You are carrying an incredible amount of symbolic weight on behalf of great numbers of lesbians, gaymen, feminists, others. There are lots of people out there reading your books, wanting more from you, people who need and want your work. *That's* hard enough. And then you have to spend some of your professional time with people like the ones today who are scared of you and beat up on you emotionally. You get drained from friends and foes alike, everyone needing you—either to admire and follow or to beat up on. I'm asking if you realized how badly worn out you are."

"I don't know how else to do it!" I exclaimed, defensively.

"I'm not suggesting you're doing anything wrong, Carter. You're not. But you're obviously exhausted. And I consider it my responsibility to raise this with you. What might help restore your energy?"

I stared blankly at her.

"What do you need that you don't have?"

"Time," I sighed. "And space."

"Then I think one of my tasks is to help you create time and space for yourself. What do you think?"

I laughed. "It seems like such a simple need!"

"No, it's not simple in the world we inhabit."

I nodded appreciatively at her. "This is helpful. Thank you."

"I am very touched by your level of commitment to the church and to your work."

LATER IN MAY, shortly before the summer break, I arrived at Elizabeth's office with the books I'd written or edited and several scores of my photographs of two trips I'd made to Nicaragua, of a trip to Neuengamme (a Nazi concentration camp), and of the irregular ordination of women priests in 1974. I felt ready, and I wanted to talk about how I had really felt about various significant political and spiritual moments in my life.

"I want to know how all of this is connected . . . how all of this is connected in me!" I announced. "And our work together is just the place for this to happen!"

"For what to happen?" Elizabeth asked.

"For me to see and feel more deeply the connections between and among all these 'isms'—sexism, racism, anti-Semitism, the work of justice, being a feminist and a lesbian, teaching theology, being christian, et cetera. I need to understand how it's all connected for me. In fact, that's what I believe this therapy's all about."

"What makes you think that?"

"Because what we're doing here is, basically, *spiritual* work together. Don't you think so?" I queried.

"What do you mean by 'spiritual?'"

"Well, the sacred Spirit *links* us, our lives, yours and mine, with all that has happened, Elizabeth—in Nicaragua, in Germany, here in the U.S., everywhere. I want to know more fully what this has meant to my life, how it's shaped me, and what it may mean for the rest of my life. It's all very, very important to me!"

Elizabeth grinned. "I think you're right about spirituality. You know, I've always believed this office is a sacred place."

"It certainly is! It's better than church!" I laughed.

Elizabeth threw her head back and laughed, too. "I agree with you about what we're doing here, and I must tell you how exciting I find our work together. I've never had anyone in here before who was more committed to making the connections between the world and the psyche. It's very exciting for me, too."

"How wonderful! I believe it's the most important work we have to do. Not just me, but *you,* too. I mean, not *you* any more than anyone else. It's the most important work we *all* have to do. And it's what psychotherapy should be all about, isn't it?"

"I certainly will try to participate in this with you. It's a very new thing we're doing here, you know."

I assumed Elizabeth meant that the making of political and spiritual connections in psychotherapy was unusual, at least in her experience. I believed her when she said it was exciting for her. I sensed that it was. In fact, it seemed to me that she was coming to life with me, that my renewed energy was tapping hers, and hers, mine. As the spring neared its end, I looked forward to therapy more than anything else in my life at the time. I had found a wellspring from which to draw deeply.

In early June, during the last session before the summer break, I took Elizabeth a series of poems I'd written to her during the last two months—"Transference Poems," I called them, quick to put a clinical tag on them myself before she could. *Transference*, unconscious emotional connections between current relationships or situations and those from our past, is a dynamic in all significant human interactions. It is a part of good therapy—but only a part, and a temporary part, if the therapy really is effective. Transference is a dynamic from which we can learn much about ourselves, our histories, and our relationships, but in order to do this, we must pass through it and move beyond it. In psychotherapy, the movement beyond transference is possible only if both client and therapist can pass through the fear that impedes the transformation of any transference dynamic into a bond of more genuine human intimacy.

I knew I was in a "transference" with Elizabeth during the second and third month of therapy because I was so idealizing her: she seemed to me, in the spring of 1987, to epitomize the woman I had always wanted to be: serene, wise, and compassionate. She was like a good mother, big sister, best self.

TRANSFERENCE

I am by patriarchal profession
a thinker and so I know
enough to know that this is
not a love poem

i feel so grateful so unspeakably
tender towards you and a disquieting
eroticism

I know enough to know
that I do
not want to sleep
with you
(although I do)

i am obsessed with you
and with myself and utterly
preoccupied with my obsession

I know enough to know
that I am
not falling
in love with you

but i am drawn to you
as helplessly as an abused child
might desire her mother

It's not your body
or soul

I want
but your presence
  in feeling my way
  through this rage and fear
    which wash my cluttered bodyself
  even as i write this
    not-a-love-poem
    to someone i cling to
      for life.

"I've written you some poems," I announced, quickly moving them as far away from her as I could.

"Do you really want me to see them?" she laughed. "You look like you're trying to hide them!"

"I'm embarrassed," I said.

"About what?"

"They're so intense. Filled with such feeling. Such pain and love. I realize it's all transference."

"Yes, you're probably right," Elizabeth concurred, "although, as I've said before, it seems too early in our work to be a transference. Transference usually happens later in psychotherapy."

"Well, I think I'm about through it, actually!" I continued.

"Through it?"

"Yes, this process is happening so fast. It all has to do with my discovering—really recovering—a powerful connection to the sacred Spirit. My pain has to do with my having denied my own connection to the Spirit. I have come to value you enormously, really to love you, for helping me begin to see this—helping me see this power, slow down with it, feel it deeply. I think my idealization of you is about done. I feel like we're moving together toward something more real."

"You've done an amazing amount of work in a very short period, Carter. You know that."

"Yes. And I thank you. I feel like we have an unusually strong bond. Do you?"

"Yes. It's a very special and joyful connection. I admire you, Carter."

"And I admire you, too. You have been a Godsend to me."

DAWNING

My God!
Slowly coming out
of this critical sleep
I see that of course
you do not like Reagan
or the contras or the Pope
or patriarchal religion

You are too much
a sister too deeply
a soulmate

There is too strong
a spiritual link here
(which is clear to me
though without its details)

I see now

We are standing
together
in our roles
despite these roles

beyond our roles
on common ground

And it is good

Throughout the spring, Beverly Harrison, my lover and partner of seven years at the time, had been concerned about me, my exhaustion and pain. Bev believed that I needed rest and space in my life at least as much as therapy, probably more. She had assumed for a long time that the church was the primary source of emotional violence in my life and had encouraged me to take seriously how beaten up I'd been in my church work. Bev had met Elizabeth Farro in April when she'd come with me to a session. Because I had raved so about Elizabeth, Bev had been surprised to discover that she was small—a short, stocky, rather shy, hazel-eyed woman with shoulder-length, ash-blond hair— rather than a six-foot athlete with a head of blazing red curls, snapping brown eyes, and a spirit to match. Bev had been impressed by Elizabeth's warm, thoughtful demeanor and by her apparent concern for me. She had liked her and was supportive of the work I was doing with her.

Still, we were early in recovery together, struggling with our own relational dynamics, and Bev was aware of how much of my life energy, erotic and relational, as well as my money, was being poured into therapy. She also suspected that I was falling in love with Elizabeth. She knew that this happens in therapy and believed that this sort of attachment can be an important healing resource and also that it can reflect a genuine, mature bond, not merely a transference. So Bev was both grateful to Elizabeth for her work with me and feeling increasingly invisible herself—"like the wallpaper" in my life, she would say several months later when we began couples therapy.

I had not said much in therapy about Bev's and my relationship. It had not felt to me like "the problem," which I assumed to be more related to the church's violence against women and, possibly, to some childhood wound or neglect. I did feel, however, that Bev and I needed to be working on communicating with each other more spontaneously and honestly. It seemed to me that our relationship, like many long-term partnerships, was suffering from a lack of purposeful attentiveness to *us*—our feelings, dreams, fears, hopes, places of convergence and divergence. Emotionally, the relationship with Bev, increasingly through our drinking years, had felt lonely to me. It is of course lonely to be relating from inside a bottle to someone else in a bottle. And although Bev and I had been sober together for a year, it still felt to me as if we were sealed off from one another in our souls.

Bev Harrison is a luminary in the world of social ethics, feminist theory and theology, and theological education. She is esteemed and beloved by several generations of liberation theologians and feminist ethicists. Once her student, I had become an intimate friend through shared consciousness-raising endeavors in the early 1970s at Union Theological Seminary in New York City. A decade later, as her marriage came to an end, and after the completion of my doctoral studies, she and I had become lovers and, we assumed, life-partners. We had had an extraordinarily mutual and creative relationship through our work, travel, friendships, animal companions, recreation, and sex play, but we increasingly had been losing touch with each other and others through our alcoholism and, in my case, bulimia. We both knew, by the time we quit drinking through AA, that recovery was our only hope, both as individuals and as two women who loved each other.

"You *are* committed to Bev, aren't you?" Elizabeth had inquired rather sternly earlier in the spring when I had mentioned my attraction to someone else.

"Yes," I responded, "but that doesn't mean we aren't drawn to other people."

"What *does* it mean then?" Elizabeth pressed me.

"It means that Bev and I want to spend our lives as partners. We love each other. That won't end. I often say, 'Bev and I want to grow old together,' and that is to me our commitment."

"I see." She sounded unconvinced.

AT THE BEGINNING of each summer, Bev and I needed time and space together, given our respective winter lives. With Bev teaching in New York and I in Cambridge, and both of us traveling a lot, lecturing and leading workshops, we were seldom together. The summer of 1987 was no exception. We needed it, but this time I was emotionally somewhere else—in therapy, with Elizabeth, with whom I was experiencing an emotional intimacy that felt new to me. And although I, too, had assumed in April and May that my feelings of "in-loveness" toward Elizabeth were, basically, a transference and, thus, were more about my deepest spiritual yearnings than they were about Elizabeth, I was not so sure about this once Bev and I got to Maine in early June. I began to sense that Elizabeth's and my bond was *not* simply a transference, but had another, very real basis.

I wrote to Elizabeth from our summer place on Deer Isle and told her that I had begun to suspect that my feelings for her were more than simply those of transference. I explained what I meant. I wrote that, in addition to the transference I was experiencing—a childlike need to lean on her like a mother for a while—"there is something else at work between us, a wonderful, spirited dynamic moving us both, it seems to me, more fully into ourselves, empowering us."

I told Elizabeth that I believed this deeper, stronger relational current was carrying me swiftly beyond transference into something more real, mutual, and sisterly. I said that I really *did* think I was falling in love with her and that I hoped this would not scare her.

"It does not mean we have to be lovers," I said, "but rather that we have a sacred healing resource in our erotic power."

Soon after sending her this letter, I sent Elizabeth a poem about an experience I was having. Through recovery, prayer, and meditation, I was beginning to experience the real presence of Sophia, the sacred figure of Wisdom that the church has so terribly disregarded. I was becoming aware of her presence near me, though I was not sure at the time who, or what, she was. I enclosed a note with the poem.

On June 12, as I was meandering through the lupine, I had an immensely engaging "conversation" with an image—an old Sophia-type woman, much like me but older, darker, and a traveler further in every direction than me. She is more than me, more than anyone. And though she is much like me, she is much like you as well and much like a number of women I've known, loved, learned from, and taught. A more traditional Christian might say that on June 12 I prayed, or perhaps even that I encountered God in the person of Mary as Black Madonna or something of the kind. I don't know. . . .

I'm choosing now to take a step away from traditional Christian worship for a while and explore my spirituality in other ways, therapy being chief among them for the time being. . . .

I don't know who or what this lady in the lupine was or is, except that she is good for me and represents in some essential way all that I cherish and celebrate and yearn for in myself and for others too.

IN THE LUPINE

out the window
last August
i saw you, and again

in January, moving
between the white birches
which frame the field and
the high grass which
in June becomes the lupine
lavender lovely pink
white sturdy
wild and
irrepressible flower.

in August you were younger
than today and more confident
it seemed to me than anyone
i had known
(least of all myself)

you had my eyes
and laugh
and motioned me
to join you
strolling through
the tiger lilies
and heliotrope
which i did.

an image
of serenity you were
no cheap beauty but
all i imagined
a god could be

darker than me
closer to black

you told me through your green
gaze that you are
not a priest
(more like a priestess, perhaps,
though that
diminutive and derivative
term did you no justice,
nor me either).

i pondered you
and in January
saw you again
wrapped in gray wool
holding a beige lamb
in one arm the other
tucked into your shawl.

you seemed not to see
me then but i cannot forget
the way you snuggled the lamb
close to your breast
in safety.

in January i cried
so much and slept
and slept but got only more
and more exhausted.

and now
in the lupine
you are older blacker
in baggy jeans T-shirt headband
polyester jacket and lots of grey

hair you, woman, are attentive
to me inviting me close
to your body, bent and strong,
your movements deliberate
slow your face handsome
open

your smile is
knowing
though enigmatic
and i see today
your hands are
free and your power
available to me
if i dare.

A week or so later, I drove to Cambridge to meet with Elizabeth, as I would also in July and August. When I arrived, she said she'd gotten my poem and my letter.

"I think we should talk about the letter," she said when I sat down.

"You mean about my being in love with you?"

"Yes."

"I'm not sure what else to say, other than that it's a very strong feeling and very real. I'm very sexually attracted to you."

"Thank you for telling me this, Carter. I appreciated your letter. It was very courageous. It's important that you shared all of this with me." She paused. "You know and I know that if we were to have a sexual relationship, it would be abusive."

"Yes, I know." And I added, "It was hard to tell you."

She smiled and nodded. After another brief pause, she asked, "Don't you want to know if I feel the same way about you?"

"Yes, I guess so."

"Well, I don't," she stated emphatically.

"Don't what?"

"I'm not in love with you and I'm not sexually attracted to you." She paused again. "How do you feel about that?"

I didn't believe her. But I said, "I guess I'm relieved."

"Relieved?"

"Yes. It means I can stay in therapy with you."

Elizabeth looked puzzled.

"If you were in love with me or sexually attracted to me, I guess we couldn't work together, right?" I asked.

"Right," she nodded.

"Well then, I feel good!"

"Good? Aren't your feelings hurt at all?"

"Oh, I'll get over it!" I laughed.

We then changed the subject—to the work I had begun on what I had named my "Sophie journal." I began telling Elizabeth what an emotionally painstaking process this was for me, remembering Sophie, the free-spirited, imaginary girlchild who had lived in my soul once upon a time.

Sophie was my first image of God, a feisty African American (in those days in the South, we said "colored") girl who became my best friend. She first came to me in the context of my loneliness. By *loneliness,* I mean a sense of being emotionally disconnected from others—white from black, child from parent, and, as I would experience later, in adulthood, drunk from drunk (that is, myself from other addicts). Nobody listening well. Nobody being heard.

My early years were not, in the popular sense, "abusive." Like my relationship with Elizabeth would become, these early years were molded more by fear than a terrible, explicit violence. Like my parents and grandparents, I was shaped in part by a fear of loss, fear of intimacy, fear of sitting quietly with others or alone with myself. This fear formed my family dynamics much as it had the entire white, racist, middle-strata southern christian culture.

In our family, there was much love, much genuine caring for and advocacy of one another. I was a wanted child, in whom my parents delighted. But as a family, we had few emotional resources for a cultivation of serenity. Neither parent had much self-confidence or much reason for it, both having been shaped by prevailing gender, race, and class expectations. They were a "normal" white, middle-strata man and woman, though considerably more deeply rooted spiritually, kinder, and, in many ways, more courageous than lots of their peers or mine. My father worried about how the bills would be paid; my mother was afraid of her passion, her own creative energy. As their first (and, for six years, only) child, I absorbed both their love and their anxiety, their delight and their fear.

Into the midst of this world of my childhood came my imaginary friend Sophie to tell me we are *not* disconnected and that we need not be afraid of ourselves and one another. She said we are put here to create a world that is very different from the one we know best, the one that has been built on fear.

your tenacity is irrepressible, luminous, frightening. it is also my lifeline. encourage me to sit with you.

you know that i can love your sacred power only because you meet me as a sister. if you had to control me, to harness my passion or deny your own, i could not stay for long. i could not submit to such spiritual tyranny and respect either you or myself very much.

i tell you this because i respect you and love your presence in my life. otherwise, i'd gladly hand the power over to you and you could be my "god" forever. it might be easier for us both and safer. but it would not be true to who you are or who i am when i am with you.

you taught me this as we ate the raspberries we were supposed to be picking for mama's dessert. i was a child and you, Sophie, the spark of light and life within me, were teaching me self-respect and justice and the love of God.

"Why have I begun to remember Sophie in such detail and joy?" I asked Elizabeth out loud, and then I answered my own question. "Because I have begun to take time to feel my feelings, to meditate. Time and space."

As I was elaborating on Sophie and all that she represented for me, Elizabeth suddenly spoke, as if out of nowhere, with urgency:

"Carter, if we were to have a sexual relationship, it would be *chaos! Chaos!* Do you understand? You have enough chaos in your life!"

I was astonished and stared at her. "Yes," I nodded, "it would be chaos."

Over a period of a few seconds, she seemed to rearrange her sitting posture and recompose her facial features. Then she looked at me as if no one, neither she nor I, had spoken.

I PONDERED THIS all the way back to Maine and recorded it in my journal. What was going on? It was clear to me that Elizabeth was sexually drawn to me in a way that had overwhelmed her in that one moment. Why then had she lied to me?

I wrote to myself, "I have come to love her deeply as a sister who needs confidence in herself. Her openness to me in this period of spiritual awakening is the most important healing resource in my life at this time. I hope I can be helpful to her too. She seems so afraid of the erotic energy between us."

THAT SUMMER ON Deer Isle, I was filled with such yearning to continue what I seemed to have begun with Elizabeth. But what was the root of my yearning?

Like many girls in patriarchy (those who have not lost themselves even earlier through violence), I had lost myself in adolescence—my voice, my heart, my mind, my sense of amazing connectedness with the whole created earth. I had lost Sophie, my childhood spirit-friend, core of my being as a free-spirited womanchild. Without Sophie, I was essentially without myself. This had not been my mother's fault or my father's. No one person or event was to blame. The loss of my sense of self as an irreplaceable participant in the relational processes of creation and liberation was the effect of female socialization in hetero/sexist, racist, classist patriarchy.

When, because my family couldn't afford them both, I had had to give up horseback riding in order to take dancing lessons; when, in the sixth grade, the girls had had to stop playing football and instead jump rope; when I had begun to feel like I wasn't pretty enough and to worry about getting fat and to think my mouth was too big and my smile too wide; when I had begun to imagine that my teeth were bucked and ugly, that my laugh was too loud, and that I was too big to be a girl; when I had begun going to church *daily* and confessing my desire to be touched sexually; when I had begun to say prayers, and mean them, about "not being worthy to gather up the crumbs under [god's] table," something in me had seemed to die, and I had begun to feel deeply pained at this loss. Sophie, my free-spirited girl guide, had seemed to die. Now in my early 40s, I was meeting Sophia again—through sobriety, friendship, work, political resistance, play, and psychotherapy.

I had a strong sense that Sophie was with me now, everywhere, but especially in therapy. She was with Elizabeth and me as our healing Spirit. I had been at first unaware of what this strong spiritual presence was, mistaking her for a clinical transference or for the romantic state of being in love. *In fact, Sophie was with Elizabeth and me, as she is always among us, as our power to connect mutually, in a spirit*

of friendship, of sisterly and brotherly love, erotic in her passion and cre-
ativity, nonabusive in her desire.

Until the summer of 1987, I had failed to remember Sophie very well, and I still was not entirely sure what she was doing in my therapy. But Sophie was clear: she was in my relationship with Elizabeth not to be "treated" but to be liberated with us, by us, and through us. This became increasingly apparent to me as I worked on my Sophie journal.

O, Sophie, I was an only child, a lonely child, though otherwise a happy child who loved silence and found it wherever I could. I had my own life to live, my own words to speak, and you were my listening pal, hearing me to speech, source of affirmation, challenge, and humor.

You comforted me, pushed me, held me, and shook me up. You were my first love, the root of my lesbian energy and of a critical diffidence toward authority.

You urged me to feel deeply, think my own thoughts, and paint off the page.

You told me to take the space I needed to do whatever I was doing. "Don't let anyone squeeze you into a small space and try to make you invisible or negligible or thin," you warned. "Girls must be careful not to let ourselves get erased altogether!" You sounded alarmed.

But then you smiled. "I like the name 'Carter,' because it sounds like a girl who plans to take the space she needs."

You told me that feelings are the root of intelligence and creative power. "No one can tell you how to feel, but when you're close to me, you'll know," you nodded. And I did.

In the future, as in the past, I would sit with Elizabeth Farro, still and quiet, occasionally as time went on, with a red candle that I would bring, and sometimes with flowers I would pick or purchase; sitting with her, sharing silence, talking, laughing, letting the Spirit touch us both, I would know deeply in my bodyself, soul, and psyche; I would know through my feelings, intelligence, and intuition; I would know that I had met Sophie again and that she was with us now as Sophia, source of wisdom, adversary of patriarchal logic.

With Elizabeth, I was no longer a solitary girlchild with an imaginary friend, a child's image of God. I had found a sister consciously to sit with. We were working with a Spirit and a Friend who would be our wisdom if we would let her.

I see, my precious Sophie, that you have grown into Sophia for me and with me, dark source of wisdom and courage, justice and compassion, healing and anger, humor and hope. I am coming of age with you into a power that isn't mine or simply yours; but rather it is ours in relation, the power that creates and liberates, blesses and changes the world. The power of God.

I spent time in our August sessions going over the Sophie journal with Elizabeth. I had mailed it to her, along with a copy of my book *The Redemption of God: A Theology of Mutual Relation*. I had noted that I believed that the "power in mutual relation" about which I had written years earlier in this book was none other than Sophie/Sophia, and that I realized that in meeting Sophie as a child, I had indeed encountered God. I was ecstatic that I was beginning to see this, to see how immediately and intimately connected we are with and by the power of the Sacred, if only we can *see* it!

"YOU'VE TAPPED THE root of your spirituality, haven't you?" Elizabeth inquired.

"I think so, yes."

"What might this mean to your work as a priest and in the seminary?"

"I don't know, but it will change it."

"Yes, it will, Carter, in some important ways. It's essential that you give yourself a gift of lots of time and space to allow this significant change to take root. Do you agree?"

"Yes, I know you're right. The summer has helped me see this. It's been an incredible gift, this period of time away."

"You're very lucky to have it! One of the benefits of your profession."

"Indeed!"

We sat together very quietly and, it seemed to me, serenely for a minute or so.

"Elizabeth," I said, "something about *our* relationship, yours and mine, has touched very deeply my passion for mutuality as the basis of my spirituality. I literally treasure our relationship."

"How do you think our relationship has done this?"

"Well, I just have this intuition that *both* of us are, *together*, in ways we don't fully understand, being touched by what is happening here, and being changed, and that this is very good for us both."

She smiled. "You know, Carter, good psychotherapy is *always* mutual. Always a two-way process. You're very right about this. It wouldn't be good therapy otherwise."

I COULD TELL the therapy was working. By August I was *feeling* again, for the first time in recent memory, like an empowering woman-friend in relation to life itself—and especially in relation to Elizabeth. What I didn't see clearly at the time was that the healing energy in my life during the summer of 1987 was coming not only from therapy but also from slowing down, being away from work, being active in AA, resting and playing with friends, and just being in Maine.

From Maine in August, I wrote a poem and sent it to Elizabeth, who I knew, from what she had shared, was vacationing in upstate New York, somewhere to the west of us.

EMPOWERING

i bent my knees
planted my feet
among the goldenrod
looked out over
camden hills last
night and
tossed you
the sun.

like that orange
you threw my way
in bread and circus[1]
this one glistened
and sparked
roselight
as it set beyond
the lavender
mist going
your way.

not that you
don't already have
such intense heat

and friendship
but like love,
this source
of energy
must be passed
on if we're to live
at all.

so when you see
it rolling
your way over
trees hills water
scoop it up
playfully and
hold it
as a sister
carefully
and when it's
time
hurl it all
the way round
to me.

it'll come
bouncing back
amid the crystals
on jericho bay and
i'll meet it
in the water
and lift it
lightly
to the gods.

Had either Elizabeth or I been able to see beyond the flawed assumption that psychotherapy *must* locate, primarily, a childhood wound to explain every adult pain like burnout, alcoholism, or bulimia, we might have begun to realize that my therapy was nearing its end four or five months after it began as I moved toward finishing the Sophie journal, because, in fact, I had entered therapy in order to remember Sophie. But I did not yet know this.

To be sure, the summer had not been an easy time for me or for Bev. More than once, I had been shaken at the core of my bodyself in reconnecting with this remarkable source of sacred power in my childhood. I had wept a great deal and had had nightmares of being thrown off a horse, bitten by a snake, carted off to a mental hospital. At the time, I did not see that I was being *spiritually converted*, having the remnants of patriarchal logic ripped from my faith, politics, perceptions, commitments, and relationships. I feared earlier in the summer that I was having a nervous breakdown, and, in a way, I was. The logic that, in significant ways, had held my life together was breaking apart. As the Sophie journal had moved toward completion in July, my fears had begun to subside. I was being reborn.

In the late 1970s and early 1980s, I wrote poetry, prose, and a doctoral dissertation about our helping the sun to rise and our part in moving the passion and power of life itself.

Today, I believe even more strongly what I wrote then. But until I quit drinking and muddling my mind and heart, I had no lively sense of how we co-create the world. I didn't see that a little child leads us and that only she knows the way: Sophie.

She listened to my heart. She shaped my fantasies and dreams of what we'd do when we grew up—marry twin brothers, ride horses every day (mine white like me, hers black and shiny like her), and yes we'd be priests, both of us someday, women priests, handling holy mysteries.

She was the wild girlchild, the small (but not so "still") voice in me, who knew, when she heard the story of Eve and the snake and the fruit and the stupid Adam, that it was very important to take a bite from that fruit:

"Take it and eat," she instructed me. "Sure, you'll die, but you'll also live!"

And that is how it all begins, with a defiant "chomp."

By September, I had come through the turbulence of a conversion process that, in many ways, had been right beneath the surface throughout my adult life. I was ready to celebrate the spiritual power I'd recovered and recognized as sacred and as ours. I anticipated that bringing this newfound sense of freedom into my work as a priest and teacher would be challenging, and when we resumed meeting weekly in September, I told Elizabeth that I wanted to focus in therapy on important vocational and professional questions. Earlier in the summer, I had written my bishop and told him I wanted to take a sabbatical from functioning sacramentally as a priest in order to do some spiritual exploration.

Elizabeth expressed joy in what was happening to me, and in the depth of connection between us that had enabled this spiritual unfolding to take place. It was clear to me by then that my basic therapeutic work was *spiritual*, and I said so. When I asked Elizabeth what she thought, she responded that my work in therapy had moved unusually fast and that it was too soon for her to have a clear sense of what other work we might need to do together.

Although it should have ended as therapy then and there in September 1987, we went on, in our roles of client and therapist. But the therapeutic relationship had begun to be transformed for me. I knew we needed somehow to acknowledge this, and it wasn't clear to me how.

In our August session, I had spoken about my theological interest in *mutuality* and where it had originated—in my experiences, and perception, of the damaging effects of nonmutual, hierarchical, power-over relationships between groups as well as individuals. In this conversation, Elizabeth had expressed "excitement" about this topic, pointing out that there was a discussion of it in her field, too.

"Do you know about the Stone Center?" she had asked, referring to the Stone Center for Developmental Services and Studies at Wellesley College and its psychological theory of mutuality.

"No," I said.

"They're the only people I know of in psychology who're doing anything on mutuality," she said.

"I'll have to find out more about them," I agreed.

A MONTH AFTER this conversation, Peg Huff, a faculty colleague at the Episcopal Divinity School, surprised me by appearing at my office with her friend Jan Surrey of the Stone Center. After chatting for a few minutes, Jan and I agreed to meet over lunch several weeks later to discuss our shared interest in mutuality. She and I met several times during the fall of 1987 to explore our work in psychology and theology and possibilities for what would become for us a remarkable professional collaboration through the auspices of both the Stone Center and the Episcopal Divinity School.[2] Our relationship would be for us a wellspring of the very energy we were exploring together—that which I had called "our power in mutual relation," resource of what the Stone Center had termed "mutual empowerment."

Like Elizabeth and me, Jan Surrey and I were spiritually sojourning together. With Jan—Jewish, practitioner of Buddhist meditation, and sister in Twelve-Step recovery—I would be drawn close to what, as a christian, I believe the heart of God to be: the soul we share, a place of all real meeting, in which we are called forth more fully to be who we are at our best—in our authenticity and vulnerability, which is our strength.

With Elizabeth, I had begun to slow down, to hear my own most authentic voices, and to trust what I was hearing deep in my soul. Jan met me gladly in this spiritual opportunity, believing with me that *each* of our lives was being touched and transformed only because *both* were. Together we were opening more deeply into faith, an awareness of being connected not only to one another but to the larger world. We were becoming more fully ourselves in common vulnerability. We were touching our strength. This was a healing process because it was mutual and, as such, a Godsend to us both.

Our relationship would help season our spiritualities and politics, help radicalize our work in psychology and theology. Jan and I would be changing with one another through our professional ventures, meditation, walks, shared process of recovery from addiction, efforts to find adequate languages for what we were learning together, and a careful attentiveness to points of pain and longing in our respective lives—in mine at the time, to understanding more fully what was happening between Elizabeth and me.

SEPTEMBER 1987 TO JANUARY 1988:
Yearning to Be-friend

DURING THE NEXT five months, my desire to move toward the termination of therapy and allow the relationship to evolve toward friendship became paramount for me. Looking back, I see how much this had to do with my needing to trust the relational process that had brought me home to Sophia and, with Her, to myself. *Intuitively, I knew that any relationship that cannot, on principle, grow more fully mutual is not a right or trustworthy relationship.* Sophia had given me this intuition and, it seemed, had led me to Elizabeth at this time to explore it in my life. Not only did it make no good sense to me, emotionally or spiritually, that Elizabeth and I could not ever become friends, but it seemed seriously wrong that we could not. I felt as if I were facing an imminent emotional betrayal through a sister who wished to do me no harm, much as I had felt when sincere church-people had explained to me why women, or openly gay and lesbian people, could not be priests.

Bev and I were beginning couples counseling, a process that would help us hear one another's truths with less fear and, over time, would begin to clarify and secure our commitment "to grow old to-gether." As a priest, teacher, and theologian, I was discovering that, with Sophie's epiphany in my life, the church was losing its power to hurt my feelings, diminish my sense of professional value, or inhibit my erotic passion. Jan Surrey and I were beginning a creative collegial journey together at the interface of our most pressing spiritual, rela-tional, professional, and political commitments. My participation in AA and Overeaters Anonymous, along with my most intimate rela-tionships, including that with Elizabeth, had given birth to a newly forming serenity. For the first time since childhood, I was beginning to feel genuinely at home with myself.

Elizabeth had helped me find my spiritual path. It was leading me beyond the authority of the patriarchal logic of the church and, ironically, beyond the tenets of psychodynamic psychotherapy as prac-ticed by Elizabeth. I did not need to be in "treatment" with her any longer. In fact, I needed not to be. But I stayed because I didn't want to lose our spiritually evocative connection. I believed that Elizabeth didn't want to lose it either. I sensed that we were sisters together on a journey, and I wrote a poem, which I did not share with Elizabeth until much later.

MUTUALITY

in becoming
sisters
to our priests
and friends
to our
healers
we are finding
our ways
home to
our
selves.

In September, sensing the radicality of Elizabeth's ambivalence about how professional or sisterly to be with me, I told her I needed her to be *real* with me, that I couldn't stay in therapy unless she was present with me as a sister. She said she would like to be and would try. Then, looking puzzled, she said she would need my help in this process, because it was new to her.

"Hasn't any other patient ever asked you to be real with them?" I asked.

She shook her head. "No, not in quite this way."

I was touched by her candor and vulnerability.

Shortly afterward, I wrote and gave her this poem:

CONSPIRACY

if you asked how i know
you i'd say we met
somewhere beneath
the surface of our lives.

i'd say i met
you in your deep
breathing and in your
face so warm it melts
your cool restraints.
i'd say i heard
you first in your
outburst of spontaneity
and from then
on as much in your
silence as your
speech. i'd say we met
in the heart of a con-
spiracy when we began
to breathe
together.

I was unable to lay aside my desire for a friendship further down the road. "Friendship" was taking on a larger meaning, I believe, to both Elizabeth and me than the term ordinarily denotes. *In relation to Elizabeth, friendship for me had to do with the* trustworthiness *of our relationship because it signaled the authenticity of a shared commitment to a mutually empowering process—by its very definition a process of relational openness and change.* Was Elizabeth truly a sister, open and growing and changing with me? Or was this a game we were playing? Was I in a relationship? Or was I in a psychodrama *about* relationship?

"ARE YOU FRIENDS with your former therapists?" Elizabeth asked me one day when I mentioned one of them.

"Yes and no," I said. "In all three cases the door was left open to that possibility, and in all three cases they're folks I respect and love. But I see them very seldom. Hardly at all. That could always change, of course, but as it is, they live in different parts of the country and our paths don't cross very often. I wish they did. I'd like to see them."

"I see. They were *willing* to become your friends?"

"Yes."

Elizabeth appeared thoughtful.

On another occasion she asked how I decide which students will become my friends.

"I don't just *decide!* Friendship is a relational *process* that involves both people and the circumstances of our lives. I mean, I wind up being friends in life with folks whose basic values and commitments I share, or who live next door, or who work alongside me in the church or in the struggle for justice, or who walk their dogs with me."

"How often do you see your friends?" she inquired.

"Some people I see almost every day, like Sue Hiatt, my beloved sister and colleague, because she and I work together. Others, like John Craig, my wonderful friend from high school days in Charlotte, I may not see more than once every year or so, if that often. Some people I may see over coffee only once or twice in a decade, and I still experience them as friends."

"I see." Elizabeth looked as if she were pondering my words for hidden meaning.

What did I mean by friendship? What was this obsession? *It was about relational trust, about mutual authenticity as the only trustworthy relational movement.*

Entering psychotherapy, I had been not only a tired, burnt-out woman, not only a recovering alcoholic and bulimarexic woman, but I was also, to some degree at least, an intellectually engaging, emotionally accessible lesbian, feminist, priest, theologian, and teacher whose deepest passion for a long time had been a commitment to relational mutuality.

Mutuality is a way of being connected with one another in such a way that both, or all, of us are empowered—that is, spiritually called forth; emotionally *feel* able; politically *are* able to be ourselves at our best, as we can be when we are not blocked by structures and acts of violence and injustice or by attitudes and feelings of fear and hatred.[3] I could not conceal my passion for mutuality in order to be a "good client." I couldn't function in a make-believe relationship. I *had* to know my sister-healer—how she felt, where she stood, what she believed, what her life was like as it pertained to mine. The truths of our lives—my life, in this case—could be discerned only in a genuinely mutual context. This I believed.

How did Elizabeth feel about racism? What had *she* gone through as a lesbian in her work? What did *she* make of the Reagan phenomenon? Had *she* ever been to Nicaragua or elsewhere in the two-thirds world? What did the Holocaust mean to *her*? Was *she* christian or had she ever been? Did *she* celebrate Easter, the solstice, or other days of festivity and sacred meaning?

If therapy is a process that helps folks learn to be more fully present in the world, more fully ourselves, why would a client not expect her therapist to engage questions drawn from deep within her soul? It was to me spiritually *essential* that, in therapy, I be part of a mutually transformative process, not plopped on a couch in front of an "automatic teller" that had been programmed in medical school to be kind and empathic. I believed then, and believe even more now, that *all* psychospiritual healing—not some, all—is steeped in unpretentious, honest, relational participation in which we share stories and experiences; compare notes and notice differences; disagree, collide, and compromise; seek ways through impasses; and are delighted, sad, sorry, and excited *with* one another.

Elizabeth tried to respond to me in this way, but increasingly it seemed to scare her. And when it did, she would speak of her belief in the importance of boundaries and, at times, would scold me as if I were a bad girl who didn't respect her boundaries the way she expected her patients to respect them.

And I was increasingly insistent, "pushy": Have *you* ever had this experience? Have *you* felt this way? What do *you* think about what I've just shared with you? Has this kind of thing ever happened to *you*? How do *you* feel when . . . ? Tell me what it's like for *you* in your practice when someone says something like this. . . .

I was not expecting full "self-disclosure" by Elizabeth any more than I do in *any* authentic, mutually respectful relationship. I needed her to meet me as a sister because that is, in fact, who she was to me—and I knew intuitively that Elizabeth Farro knew that this was true, and that ours was a healthy, good connection.

FAITH

you say
you're not sure
we can move
beyond our
clinical beginnings.

i say
this is
a crock.

you say
i'm probably
right but
you'd have
to be

100%
sure.

i say
lady
where's your
faith in
the power
already
transforming
us
both?

One day I told Elizabeth that she seemed very frightened at the possibility of letting a friendship grow between us.

"Not frightened, cautious," she responded.

"Is this the first time a patient has ever asked you about this?" I asked.

"No," she said. Then, after a pause, "But it's the first time I've seriously considered becoming friends with a former patient."

"Well, I think the rule that forbids friendship between therapists and former patients is a crock," I stated.

She nodded. "I'm not sure you're wrong about this."

"So," I asked, "can we talk about this ridiculous rule?"

"Let's talk about what you mean by friendship and why it means so much to you," Elizabeth responded.

"It means so much to me because it has to do with everything I hold as sacred. I'd be glad to share with you what I'm writing these days about mutuality," I said. "I'll be glad to discuss anything you want and I'd love to and share with you poems and other pieces I'm working on about this issue between us."

"That would be helpful to me," she replied. "It's important that I understand why friendship means so much to you."

"Elizabeth, I can't understand how, knowing me, you can imagine that I wouldn't want us to be friends!" I felt frustrated, hurt, and puzzled.

Elizabeth looked puzzled, too. "But you don't need any more friends, Carter. You have lots of friends."

The passion on my part for a relational authenticity that could become whatever it was meant to become and Elizabeth's ambivalent response were becoming the *driving force* of our relationship. Had I not come so rapidly to love her, to experience an empathy and bondedness with Elizabeth in her ambivalence and my passion, perhaps I would have seen that our relationship, for all its value, could not continue to work *as psychotherapy*, given Elizabeth's investment in professional boundaries and my insistence that she meet me as a sister. We were working increasingly at cross-purposes.

In order to stay connected to Elizabeth, I had begun within the first two months of therapy to conceal the extent to which her ambivalence was hurting me. Our relationship was mirroring the fear and rejection I long had experienced in the church, academia, and larger society by those who do not look kindly upon passionate, free-spirited women and girls. I think that neither Elizabeth nor I realized that, in this therapeutic context of fear and ambivalence, I was beginning a descent into the fear and pain that had been the root of my abuse of alcohol and food.

I wrote another poem to Elizabeth and shared it with her.

CRUCIBLE

can we
keep the fire

hot enough to transform
us both and cool
enough to shape us
into who we are
becoming?

we must be
patient with
one another

In October, I rented the video of *One Flew over the Cuckoo's Nest* and watched it alone one night. I had felt for some reason that I had to see it again, after many years. The next day I told Elizabeth I had been deeply moved by the beautiful, silent Native American man's leaping out the window at the end and running freely away from the hospital.

"That's what I think we should do, Elizabeth."

"What?"

"Run freely away from this psychiatric structure that is preventing our relationship from growing or changing in ways that would be good for us both. Really, I feel like this structure—therapy—is beginning to strangle the life out of me, and I sense it's doing the same to you."

Elizabeth said nothing.

"I'm not asking you to make a dramatic break from your profession, but rather to be open with me to the future. I need this from you. And I wonder if you need it too."

"Why, Carter? Why do you need this from me?"

"Because our work has begun to hurt me. And because I've grown to love you as a sister and I sense you feel much the same way about me."

Elizabeth was silent for a while. Then she spoke, but not exactly to me. She seemed to be speaking into the air, perhaps to herself: *"We could be friends, you and I, if . . . "* She did not complete the sentence.

"If *what?*" I asked.

Elizabeth said nothing, and her face seemed to me expressionless.

"If *what*, Elizabeth?!" I was pushing at her. "We could be friends *if what?*"

She turned her face away from me as if I hadn't spoken and said nothing, and I retreated into the silence with her, though my heart was thumping.

Soon I gave her another poem.

UNFOLDING

*if i believed
i'd not see you
again not light
a candle with you
again not look
you in the eye
again wondering
what's happening
to you as well
as me not laugh
with you again
i'd fold up
a small piece*

of my heart
and a larger piece
of my soul
and tuck them
away in a file
marked
"broken."

as it is
my heart and
soul are
unfolding
and what was
broken is
becoming
whole
again.

In late October, during a week-long conference in New York with other women theologians, I wrote Elizabeth a letter saying that it seemed to me it was time for my therapy to move toward closure and for us to begin working on a transition either into a friendship or toward ending the relationship altogether. I tried to explain why I felt this way—that our work had been wonderful, but that therapy was really over. I felt that something else, a freer dynamic, was struggling to be born between us.

When I arrived for my session the following week, Elizabeth looked angry.

"Are you angry?" I asked.

"Not angry. Just a little annoyed and surprised."

"By my letter?"

"Yes, by your letter."

"What annoyed you? My asking you to reconsider becoming friends?"

"No. Your having decided to end therapy. This seemed to me, Carter, to come out of nowhere, very unilaterally. You talk about mutuality and then write a letter announcing your decision to end. This doesn't seem very mutual to me."

"I'm sorry. I guess I was trying to get a conversation going, not announce an already-made decision."

"I see. Well, you sound more open to discussing it now than you did on paper, at least as I read you."

"You may be right. I may have come on strong with my conviction that it's about time for us to either end or change. But I *do* believe this is true, Elizabeth."

"Carter, we've only been working together for eight months! This may be just the *beginning*. We don't know yet what we may discover that needs attention."

"Elizabeth, I don't think there *is* anything else. No hidden, mysterious place."

"You may be right." She nodded.

"Do *you* think there is?"

"I don't know, of course. I do know that you mentioned several months ago having been molested by a man who worked for your family, and we haven't explored this. *That* seems to me fairly important."

"Well, we can explore it if you want to, but I'm not sure what there is to explore."

"I'm not either. But I think we need to look at it at some point."

"That would be fine."

"In the meantime, I ask you, Carter, to allow this to be as mutual a process as we can make it. Mutuality means a lot to me and I know it does to you. It would be very sad if we got derailed because one of us were acting unilaterally."

"I agree."

O Sophia!

those who touch and transform us are, like you, moved and changed with us.

and what blessing in knowing that, in opening ourselves, we inspire others to open with us. in daring to receive love, we enable them to give. in the courage to be healed, we become healers—and never apart from those we heal.

this mutual co-inherence, the essence of healing and liberation for us all, has managed to escape the patriarchal logic of both western medicine and christianity. small wonder we are so sick, so broken, so badly in need of you.

topple our lives and bear with us through the chaos of your coming. in your love, make us conscious of the things we don't see.

I often would call Bev at night and tell her what had transpired in therapy. I spoke again and again of Elizabeth's and my sitting on the floor together, sometimes working with a candle between us, engaged mutually in an empowering, spiritually evocative process. Bev was amazed!

"I can't believe Elizabeth Farro has any qualms about being a friend of yours further down the road," she asserted. "It sounds to me like you're *already* friends. Either that, or the woman is a consummate actress and a fraud, in which case you're going to be very badly hurt and I'm going to be very angry."

As Thanksgiving neared, I wrote this poem and sent it to Elizabeth.

LOBOTOMY

if you reject me as
the friend i want
someday to be i
hope i can sustain
the grief for the
rest of my life.

but please hear
me: this is not my
worst fear, which is
that sooner or later
the heat of my
passion will have
been so diminished
by the master's tools
that i'll have become
well-enough adjusted
to live a lukewarm
life.

i'd rather leave
in rage and hatred,
madwoman at the core,
than with gratitude
for your help in

containing my
passion for justice
and friendship and us.

On we went, Elizabeth and I. I would mail her my poems and bring up the subject—"the 'f' word"—from time to time, but we seldom would discuss the poems or my books. She would not bring them up, perhaps because therapists don't often initiate conversations. And I would not bring up what I had written for fear of being experienced, yet again, as "pushy."

We'd talk about other things as they'd come up, like Bev's and my having Thanksgiving dinner with Diana, a friend of ours who was dying, and with her spouse; about my deceased father's birthday and Diana's death the next day; about how I was feeling in the midst of this death, grief, and memory. But each topic and intense feeling—about death, love, loss, grief, and about the power of friendship and the presence of loved ones—would bring me back to Elizabeth's and my relationship and the possibility that it simply would end. Just like that. The possibility that the sister whom Sophia had sent to meet me, to call me forth, to hear me to speech, would simply disappear and be gone from my life. Not by death and not really by choice, but because of a rule shaped professionally out of white men's fear of losing control.

ELIZABETH HAD SAID that we would not be friends unless she changed her mind. One day she said she wanted to be my friend, but couldn't because it would involve risk. "There is always a possibility that it would harm you, Carter. I would have to be 100 percent sure that it wouldn't and since we can't be 100 percent sure of anything, I could not risk this."

To which I responded, "Relationships involve risk, Elizabeth! Loving, caring, creating, being human, involves risk. *Neither* of us can guarantee there would be no harm between us. *But that's true of therapy as well as friendship.*"

I was angry, hurt, and reluctant to let Elizabeth know how angry and hurt I was, for she had said to me that she did indeed feel "pushed" by me toward friendship, and that she didn't like it.

"I'M A PERSON who changes, Carter," she told me at another time. "I may change my mind about friendship."

"Will you let me know if you do?"

"Of course!" she laughed.

"That would be wonderful!"

"Yes, it would," she agreed.

"In the meantime, is it helpful to you to be reading what I'm writing about friendship—I mean, my poems and books?" (At my suggestion, I was paying Elizabeth by the hour to read the materials I sent her, or as much of them as she could or wanted to, up to two hours of reading per week.)

"Yes, it is. I'm touched by the time and effort you're putting into this."

"Well, I'm working on some pieces for you—actually, some art, which I won't be able to finish by Christmas, but also some written reflections on love, mutuality, and other images of friendship, which I'll send you as a Christmas present!"

"Great!" Elizabeth laughed.

OVER THE CHRISTMAS holidays, I mailed Elizabeth the gift: a homemade book of images about friendship, which I called "christmas images." I was trying to help her become real with me and to tell her as honestly as possible who I was in relation to her. I wanted to assuage her fear:

PHANTASIE

How can I be tender enough
with you,
when words like "love"—
these words, my words,
and ours, the words of
our language—
are so freighted with
prepackaged meanings
and stir such fear?

How can I speak to you of love,
my therapist, and at least in my Phantasie,
my good, soulful friend-in-the-making,
without intruding? Can I risk offering
such words as a gift and blessing, to comfort
rather than to frighten or offend?

FRIEND

It's beyond therapy, yet it has moved through the therapeutic
process. Like a swift, deep current in a major river, the therapy
has been a "moment" between us, moving us to reassess
what I/we have learned to believe about healing and its connect-
edness to possibilities of friendship—mutuality—relationship
in which both (or all) persons can become more wholly
our Selves.

a good
   friend
is a
   comforter,

one with whom
we draw strength
one who strengthens/
is strengthened

TRANSFERENCE

you become sometimes mother to the child within me and sav-
ior to the helpless little one I am when I feel alone and afraid.
These are "moments," even in the therapeutic situation, into
which I move and out of which I emerge—and I see them, feel
them, and realize them, such moments, throughout my life.

I also know deeply and well that in any "moment" I
could mother you or be your priest (not that you would want a
priest!)—The relational power between us is being sifted into
mutual measure, which is all for the good.

SOULMATE

we are holy-grounded, *standing together in*
this place

i consider a tree
a sister, a friend,

standing with me/us
on this earth—

a soulfriend sees
in the tree the same
life spark
and
never ceases to be
grateful, and
amazed!

Remembering the Violence

FOLLOWING THE HOLIDAY break, I told Elizabeth I needed to know where she was now in considering the possibility of friendship. Had my Christmas writings been helpful to her?

Elizabeth said she had appreciated what I had written and that she had thought a lot about my desire for us to be friends. She paused for a moment, then said she had decided she could not be. She said she was very sorry, that she wished it could be different. She appeared to be deeply pained. I was quiet for a few moments, then began to cry. I glanced at Elizabeth and saw she was crying, too.

"I'm sorry," I said after a few moments, "but I can't stay in therapy any longer, given your decision. It's just not the right place for me to be. This is hurting me too much."

"I'm sorry you feel that way," she responded.

We sat quietly for a few minutes, both of us in tears. "Do you understand *why?*" I asked. "Why the possibility of our becoming friends has been so important to me? Why I can't stay?"

"No, I don't understand, Carter." She shook her head.

"Then I feel like I've been speaking and writing to a wall!" I snapped angrily. I threw a wad of paper at her as I spoke.

"Do you always act like this when you don't get your own way?" Elizabeth snapped back.

I shook my head. "I don't know. Maybe so. I don't think so, but maybe so." Tears were streaming down my face. "I feel awful," I cried.

"About what?"

"I don't know. I'm in such pain and I don't know why. I keep wondering what I'm doing to cause you to react to me this way."

"What way?"

"So angrily."

"I'm not angry, Carter."

"Well, what *are* you then?"

"I'm frustrated."

"At me, right?"

"I'm frustrated that you will not accept no for an answer. I have said it repeatedly and you keep pushing me about friendship."

"Elizabeth, you asked me to help you understand what I mean by friendship. You told me that my writing is helpful to you. You asked me to help you be real with me. I'm just trying to be myself in response to you."

"And that's exactly why I asked you if you always act like this when people disagree with you or don't give the answer you want. Are you simply being yourself when you throw things at people who cross you?"

"For God's sake, Elizabeth, it was just *paper!* I'm sorry. I don't mean to be pushing you. I'm not trying to have my own way. I'm trying to figure out how to be in this relationship. How to be myself without terrifying you."

"You don't terrify me, Carter."

"Well, without freaking you out."

"You could try showing me a little respect."

"You don't feel like I *respect* you, Elizabeth? I can't believe it!"

"Not when you're pushing at me, Carter."

"I guess you and I understand 'respect' very differently. I *do* respect you. If I didn't, I wouldn't give a damn about being your friend."

SEVERAL DAYS LATER, Lane, a sister priest, and I were in my living room discussing work-related matters when I burst into tears. Lane looked at me kindly, knowingly.

"Is it about Elizabeth?" she asked. From time to time, I had shared with her some of the written materials I'd sent Elizabeth. Lane was a splendid pastor whose psychological instincts I trusted. She had heard my pain about therapy on more than one occasion.

"Yes. I'm just so confused. I don't understand this pain. Why am I hurting so?"

"Carter, I know you care about Elizabeth, but she's abusing you. I daresay she's not meaning to, but she is."

I was sobbing.

Lane continued, "I think she's scared to death of the intimacy she's experiencing with you. If she won't consider becoming a friend after therapy, given what she obviously feels for you, then there's something the matter here. Quite frankly, I think you should quit therapy."

I knew Lane was right. I was torn between believing that I needed to leave therapy at once and feeling like I needed to hang in with Elizabeth. I was in such pain, increasingly. What was going on? I needed to know. Was there, possibly, some hidden cause, some childhood trauma, at the bottom of my obsession with this friendship quest?

I spoke briefly about this with Cass, the therapist Bev and I were seeing, whom Elizabeth had recommended. I knew that Cass and

Elizabeth regarded each other highly as professional colleagues and that Cass was fond of me. I told Cass that Elizabeth's rigidity about boundaries and friendship beyond therapy was hurting me, and yet that I felt my therapy possibly was not over. I sensed that Elizabeth believed there might be some childhood abuse, something yet to be remembered, that would help explain why I was in such pain about the therapy relationship. I also knew that Elizabeth and Cass were consulting one another about my work.

"I think I need to be in therapy with *someone*," I reflected, "especially if I'm working on childhood abuse memories. Could you refer me to someone else?"

"I really can't," Cass responded thoughtfully. "Elizabeth is the best in the field, especially on abuse issues." She paused. "As for friendship, we therapists do things in our own way. I can't speak for her, but give your therapy a little more time, Carter."

BUT THE PAIN was too great. I decided I had to leave. The next two weeks, in late January 1988, brought much darting back and forth between my wanting to leave therapy *immediately* and a desire to do some justice to the process of closure. Even then I realized that I was trying to hold on to the relationship.

I told Elizabeth I'd like us to do a ritual for ending. She said she'd think about it and that she needed to know what I had in mind. I prepared a simple ceremony in which we invited one another to acknowledge together what was being lost, what was *not* being chosen, and to affirm what the therapy had given each of us. I went over it with Elizabeth and proposed that we do it together, as a way of ending our relationship, on Monday.

Over the weekend, however, sorrowful in my soul, I phoned Elizabeth to say that I seemed to need more time for ending and that I wanted to use the closing ritual over a number of weeks rather than in one final session. I asked how she was feeling about the ritual and about ending our relationship. She said she was not sure how she felt about the ritual and that she was very sad about ending our relationship. I said I also was feeling sad and that it seemed to me so very wrong and unnecessary. She said, "Let's talk about this when we meet on Monday."

I WAS READY to give up. I had been struggling for almost a year. Eleven months earlier, I had arrived exhausted in Elizabeth's office. Now I felt like I was breaking into pieces: there was in me, alive and kicking, the feisty, pushy Sophie, but there was also a remnant of patriarchal logic, a good daughter of the father/god, a wounded, obedient child who needed to be taken care of. It seemed to me that this was the part of me that Elizabeth felt safest with.

And so it was that on the last Monday of January 1988, as I arrived in her office, *I unconsciously made the decision to be this child.* It was the only way I could continue in therapy, the only way to be in relationship to Elizabeth. I told her I needed to find out why I was so sad about ending.

In this moment, I slipped unawares into Elizabeth's therapeutic framework, and for the first time in the therapy, I began to believe I really was in some way crazy for caring so much about this relationship. In deciding to stay in therapy, I unwittingly was giving myself over to Elizabeth's consciousness, asking her to help me understand a pain that, I felt, must surely be pathological.

"I feel better now," I said. "We're in the middle of a process that is scary to me, but I want to give myself over to it."

Elizabeth's face was radiant. "I feel joy about your decision. I hope you can trust the process between us. We can't know where it may lead us, but we both need to stay open."

Open? I wondered to myself. Whatever does she mean by "open"? Had I not been open? Had this whole painful situation not been generated by my desire for us to be open? I was in too much pain and, by then, fear to speak such questions aloud. I recorded them silently in my journal, along with the one big question that had taken hold of me: *Am I crazy?*

This question had come to haunt me again, as it had throughout my life, I would later see, whenever I was on the verge of smashing through the patriarchal logic of our religious, educational, professional, or psychological institutions: *Am I crazy?* It was a question that exhausted me, depleted and disempowered me, held me back from breaking through by holding me in fear. Or so it had in the past.

> *shame on me for eating too much drinking too much*
> *throwing up too much shame on me for being too*
> *fat too fast too busy too smart too loud too*
> *silent too assertive too shy too christian too*
> *pagan too feminist too conventional too dykey*
> *too straight too political too spiritual too*
> *lusty too passionate too much shame on me for*
> *raising issues taking offense speaking up*
> *upsetting or irritating good folks pushing hard for what*
> *i believe is not merely my opinion but the right thing*
> *to do shame on me for daring to*
> *speak up, for loving you, sacred sister, shame on*
> *me. shame on you. shame on us. for shame.*

In the early part of February, I came up with an image to help me probe what I assumed was a problem in my own psyche, but Sophie's hand was still at work in this and she was not about to turn me over to textbook psychiatry. I came up with an image of "dragons," brothers or sisters with whom I was contending fiercely, trying to establish right-relation. There were five dragons, each with a name and a visual and verbal description that I shared with Elizabeth:

There was the dragon Sigmund, stern patriarchal shrink who thinks he knows what's what and often does not. Then there was his smaller, younger, female cohort, Farro, who was too timid to stand up to Sigmund though she was, in fact, a wiser dragon. The third was Mama, a dancing dragon, so anxious about her passion, and mine. The fourth was Pushy, the high-spirited, feisty womanchild who doesn't take no for an answer. Finally, there was Jeff, the yardman who'd molested me. Jeff had not raped me, but over about a six-month period when I was five and six, he had fondled me a number of times. Since I had not understood what he was doing, or why, the abuse had left me with a very puzzling "dragon."

Each of my dragons, Sophie had suggested, was in my life to be tamed, not killed. For about a month in therapy, I wrote to them, spoke to them, and did my damndest to befriend them. Elizabeth seemed intrigued by my dragon work, and was far more receptive to my focusing on Mama, Jeff, and Pushy in my therapy sessions than on either Sigmund or, especially, Farro.

Deep in my soul, Sophie was telling me I was nearing the end of therapy. She was showing me that the befriending of the dragons was an acknowledgment that we all have our own stories, that we all have "dragons," and that, if the truth be known, we all *are* dragons who are capable of doing great harm to one another *and* of participating in one another's healing and liberation. Sophie said that our common capacity to do harm does not relieve us from being accountable for the harm that we do.

In this spirit, I was especially angry at two of my dragons, Farro and Mama. I was angry at their collusion with patriarchal power-relations. Sigmund I was ready to send out to pasture, not without some appreciation for his creativity and courage. Pushy, I had to admit, I was appreciating more and more. As for Jeff, I had always known he hadn't deserved the severe beating, the racist hatred and violence, that had come down on his body in the aftermath of his abusive treatment of me.

Are those who violate us *really* our brothers and sisters, or is this just an idealized language of a spiritual rhetoric? Was Jeff my brother? Was he *still* my brother after what he did? Was I still his little sister? And Farro—was she really my sister even if she was not to be my friend? What does it involve, taming dragons who will not befriend us? These are questions with which, thanks to Sophie, I was wrestling. These questions were my spiritual breath. They were keeping me alive.

>   *you are our vision, spirited child.*
>
>   *the pilgrimage with you into scary places is to tame the dragons, not kill them: these religious icons, professional idols, people-eaters, so contemptuous and frightful if we give them power-over us, to bless or heal, transform or liberate, anything.*
>
>   *you are our eyes, spirited child.*
>
>   *through you, we see that unless we tame the dragons, they will destroy us as surely as they will eat themselves alive in the kingdom of the dead.*
>
>   *you are our heart, spirited child.*
>
>   *this taming is a process that requires even more imagination and humor than courage! it all began for me when you insisted that i love, not worship, you.*
>
>   *you are our dream, spirited child.*
>
>   *it's been an adventure ever since, in which you spark my questions and my passion. Like lightning bugs twinkling in the night, you invite me to catch you, catch up, catch on.*

Still, I could not bring myself to leave Elizabeth.

Much earlier, about three months into the therapy, I had mentioned to her that I had been sexually molested by Jeff, the black man who did yard work for my family. I had told her that I had been inappropriately touched and had been emotionally confused, and that I had *not* been raped, sodomized, forced to perform oral sex on this man, or physically damaged. I said that I had never forgotten the trauma of witnessing this man's beating by the white police after I reported the abuse to my parents. Elizabeth and I had discussed this briefly and she had said she assumed we would need to look at this more closely at some point. In fact, she had expressed some astonishment that I had mentioned it so casually. She had told me that this abuse was likely to be more significant than I realized.

Five months into the therapy, I had also explored with Elizabeth the psychosexual effects of my father's having spanked me as a child. He had never beaten me or physically wounded me, but had used a switch or hairbrush on my bare bottom in response to my childlike proclivities for talking back or disobeying. More than once, both as a girl and as a woman, I'd experienced a confusing conflation of mildly masochistic fantasies and sexual desire. As an adult, I had become ashamed of this, and I had wanted to talk about it with Elizabeth. Early in our work together, during the summer of 1987, Elizabeth had helped me move through the shame by laughing with me about how embarrassed and hung up we get about sexual feelings and fantasies, and about how common the embodied connection is between sexual stimulation and spanking among adults who were disciplined in this way as kids. My moralisms about this happily were being laid to rest without much effort.

Looking back, I am aware that there will always be more to learn from these events if I wish to know more fully how the details of my childhood have contributed to making me who I am today.

The point is not that there was nothing else for me to feel about, or learn from, these childhood brushes with violence. *The point is that the emotionally violent character of my relationship with Elizabeth somehow "attached" itself psychologically to each of these events—the molestation and the spankings—and, over a number of weeks in the spring of 1988, both events emerged as other and larger than they had been in my life.*

In late February 1988, I awoke with a sensibility somewhere between dream and memory of having been orally sodomized by Jeff, the yardman. I could describe, in detail, what happened, and I drew a picture of it for Elizabeth. I had been terrorized. For the first time in my life, I knew, at the core of my bodyself, what it was to be raped, to fear for my life, to be unable to scream, to be able only to throw up. This, I assumed, explained my bulimia.

I didn't realize this at the time, of course, but putting myself into the framework of Elizabeth's therapeutic consciousness was paying off. I found myself believing that this childhood rape was the reason for my intense pain in therapy. I thanked Elizabeth for having borne with my obsessiveness about friendship. Sounding just like her, I heard myself saying that my "pushiness" about friendship was understandable in the context of what had happened to me as a child. Having been orally raped, my psyche had every reason to be pushing against the therapeutic process, seeking friendship as an escape from having to remember such terror. Viewing myself through Elizabeth's eyes, I saw a frightened girlchild who needed Elizabeth's professional help more than ever.

"We're not through yet," I told her as we moved toward completing my work on the rape, in early April, about six weeks after I had "remembered" it.

She nodded.

"I'm not ready to leave." I was emphatic.

"You are welcome to stay," she said.

I told her how grateful I was for her presence in my life and that I had begun to see why I loved her so much: that it was *not* simply a strong sisterly connection, but my girlchild's need to be taken care of.

In Elizabeth's eyes and in my own, I was becoming an excellent patient: a wounded, needy child dependent upon her mother for help. Eager to please. Eager not to offend. Elizabeth had been unable to relate positively to Sophie, unable to befriend the free-spirited girlchild and sister-spirited woman she had helped me tap. In relation to Elizabeth, there was little room for the fiesty, passionate, healthy Spirit I had recovered. Little room for Sophie. So, in relation to Elizabeth, I unwittingly had given Her up, not entirely, but to a large extent, in the spring of 1988.

Elizabeth had seemed absolutely fascinated by my work on the rape. She told me she was astonished and delighted by what the process between us had opened up for me.

And it was not over. No sooner had I finished working on this trauma in April than I remembered another one: being horribly, violently beaten by my father for being too pushy, too mouthy, in refusing to do as I was told. For most of the next six weeks, throughout April and much of May, I explored this event in therapy and, again, experienced my bodyself as completely immersed in the abuse I was reliving through this memory. Outside therapy, I could barely make it from day to day in my teaching and at home. I felt completely dependent upon therapy and Elizabeth.

For her part, Elizabeth seemed almost mesmerized by the work I was doing.

I had become an excellent patient.

In THE MIDST of these memory sessions in the spring of 1988, Elizabeth and I arrived at her office at the same time one morning. She'd obviously been hurrying to get back on time. After we both were seated, she smiled broadly and announced:

"I've just come from meeting Dean Harkins!" Her reference was to an appointment she'd had with the head of an interseminary committee called together to address the "problematics" of the increasing numbers of "out" lesbian and gay seminarians. I had recommended Elizabeth as a possible psychiatric consultant to the committee.

"About consulting with the committee?"

"Yes."

"Great! How was it?"

"It was fine."

"Are you going to do it?"

"I think so."

"I'm delighted!"

"Thank you for your help with this," she said, sounding pleased.

"You're quite welcome," I responded.

After a pause, she continued. "I've been asking myself whether or not to share with you what the dean and I discussed and I've decided *not* to, given the importance of clear boundaries here. It would not be appropriate."

My face fell, to which Elizabeth responded:

"I can tell you're disappointed."

"Yes."

"Well, I am *not* going to tell you." She punctuated each word.

I nodded. Another ten seconds or so passed.

"Carter, I can tell you really want me to share this with you. How do you feel about me right now?"

"I'm really pissed! I feel set up emotionally. If you're not going to tell me, then don't," I blurted out.

"But you *do* want to know, don't you?" She pressed on. "I can tell."

"Elizabeth, I am outraged!" I yelled. "You come in here and announce to me that you've seen someone I know to discuss the possibility of your doing some work that interests me a lot. This was possible because several of us women seminary professors set it up for you. We are delighted you're going to be doing this, and I for one would love to talk further with you about it and hear your questions and concerns. I know you have a thing about boundaries in therapy, and if you don't want to use part of our session for this, you can phone me tonight at home. If you don't want to do that either, okay. Then don't tell me. But what is happening here right now is hurting me. These issues are *yours*. You *want* to tell me what happened! And your professional rigidity is getting in the way. Tell me or don't tell me, but quit toying with me emotionally."

Elizabeth was stonefaced. *"I will not tell you, and we will discuss this no further. Is this clear?"*

"Yes!" I was furious.

As I WAS winding up the memory work, I decided to bring some of the art I'd collected over the years to therapy to see what conversation it might generate. Among the pieces was a splendid woodcut of a woman priest holding the communion bread above her head, a gift to me shortly after our ordination from my sister priest and beloved friend Alison Cheek.

When I showed Elizabeth the woodcut, she look startled.

"You look surprised!" I said.

"What's missing in this picture, Carter?"

I looked at it carefully for ten seconds or so. "Her mouth!" I, too, was surprised, since the picture had been hanging in my living room for over a decade without my seeing this.

"You hadn't noticed this?" Elizabeth sounded incredulous.

"No," I laughed nervously. "I can't believe it!"

"It *is* amazing! Here's a picture of a woman priest without a mouth! What does this mean to you?" she asked.

"No mouth?" I felt my gut stirring. "No *voice*. No *voice*. No *voice!*" I stated angrily.

"You're angry!"

"Yes!"

"At what?"

"The church!"

"Why?"

"Because they've taken our voices away!"

"Whose voices?"

"*Women's* voices."

"*Which* women?"

"*All* women who have anything to say that is incompatible with white male normative thinking!"

"Like you?"

"*Yes! Like me!*"

"You're angry that the church has taken away your voice?"

"Yes!" I shouted. "And I am taking it back, dammit! No more silence. None. That's what I've been learning here."

"Good!" Elizabeth slapped her hand on the arm of her chair and laughed out loud.

I did, too, from deep within my soul.

WITH THE EXCEPTION of several sessions such as this one, the entire spring of 1988 revolved for me around my work in therapy on the two violent memories. I was drained emotionally in the sessions with Elizabeth in which I attempted to "abreact"—go back in time and relive the violence. Immediately following each of these sessions came a euphoric high not unlike the "endorphic rush" I had enjoyed in the past, as a bulimarexic woman, by eating too much and forcing myself to vomit. In therapy with Elizabeth, my entire bodyself, the whole of my embodied being, in a sense, was "bingeing" on the violence, then "purging" myself of it. Immersed in pain, I was being comforted by the pleasure of immense relief.

As summer approached and the lure of Maine began to call, a puzzling psychological shift took place in me rather abruptly: the violent memories began suddenly to recede, and this piece of therapeutic work began to seem startlingly disconnected from my past and my present. It was as if I had not really experienced this violence—and yet I had, hadn't I?

This was a strange and alarming question that I could not, and would not, raise then with Elizabeth. Whatever work remained to be done on these memories and this violence would have to be done outside of the therapeutic context. This I knew intuitively, deeply, and well, thanks to Sophia's nudging at my consciousness.

And yet I did not want my relationship with Elizabeth to end. More than ever, I wanted us to be able to keep going, not in the clinical setting, but as sisters together in the world. Something about the memories, I didn't know what, made this very important.

Something about the memories hadn't been quite right, or *entirely* true. They weren't exactly "false." I had experienced, working on the floor of Elizabeth's office, in her compassionate, caring presence, an authentic trauma—an oral rape—and then another trauma, a severe beating. My life would not be the same again. My consciousness had been raised and I could never again not know the sheer first-person terror of violence against women and children. But something about the memories still needed attention—*our* attention, Elizabeth's and mine. It was as if this was why Elizabeth and I had met in the first

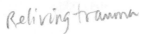
Reliving trauma

place: *to be able to keep exploring the memories, the violence, moving together toward some deeper truths about our lives as women in the world.*

This possibility was still too small and too unformed for me to realize. It was an intuition in May 1988. I could not form any coherent words around it, except *friendship,* and it made me tremble to imagine mentioning this to Elizabeth and being told no. It was too sacred. Too important. I did not know how I would be able to stay connected with this sister I had found. I found myself praying and weeping for a way to open us to this possibility.

I knew therapy had to end. For one thing, I couldn't keep paying for it. I had already borrowed most of what I had paid her, and there was no more money for this. It was also imperative that we end, formally, as doctor and patient, therapist and client, because whatever was happening between us was requiring a different basis of relationship: sister? soulmate? friend? sojourners together in a mysterious realm? Who could we be to each other? Who were we *already* with each other? Something about the memories. . . . I would not know what for almost two years, and even now as I write this book, I am not entirely sure.

As we approached the summer break, Elizabeth seemed to realize all of a sudden that we had only one or two more sessions until I'd be gone again.

"I can't believe how fast summer's come!" She sounded stunned. "You'll be gone next week! This feels too fast, too soon."

"Yes," I agreed.

There was a pause. "Aren't you going to miss me?" she asked gently and a little playfully.

"Yes. I'm going to miss you, Elizabeth, and aren't you going to miss *me?*"

She nodded.

As DURING THE previous summer, I was commuting to Cambridge from Deer Isle once a month to meet with Elizabeth. In June, I raised the question of friendship again, and again she said no.

We were at that moment sitting on the floor, a candle burning between us. I told Elizabeth that I'd had a dream in which she had refused to become my friend. I said that, in my dream, I had asked her if, as a priest, I could bless her before we terminated the therapy.

"I dreamt that you then fell to your knees in front of me, and that I asked you please to get up. 'I cannot bless you unless we are standing on the same ground as sisters and friends,' I said. 'Only in this way can I bless you.' In the dream, you refused to get up. So I got down on my knees with you, took your hands in mine, and blessed you," I reported to Elizabeth.

As I finished recounting the dream, I realized that, in the telling, I had reached out and taken Elizabeth's hands and was holding them as I spoke. I was stroking her fingers gently. "I feel like the dream has just come true, that I have in some way blessed you?" My words were more question than declaration, and I was quietly crying.

Elizabeth's face was filled with sadness, and a tear was on her cheek. "Thank you for understanding," she said.

"Understanding what?" I asked.

There was only another tear.

I pressed on. "Why you won't be my friend?"

Elizabeth nodded.

"But I *don't* understand, Elizabeth. It seems to me we are *already* friends and have been, at some level, for a long time."

IN JULY, at my initiative, we discussed our relationship for several hours. We talked about how empowering it had been for both of us, about how much we would miss each other. We meditated together. We spent a good bit of time laughing. As the session was ending, Elizabeth told me that her decision for "no friendship" was "tentative."

"That's wonderful!" I responded. "Maybe someday it will be possible for you."

She smiled.

A couple of weeks later, sitting at the water's edge in Maine, I felt inspired. For an hour or two, I wrote of how mystical and mutual the connection with Elizabeth had been from the beginning for me and, I believed, for her as well. I wrote about friendship. I believed the Spirit would, at some time in the future, bring us back together and I said so. "The Friendship Pages," as I named this document, were a spirited, audacious attempt to give voice to my passion for the connection between us:

> *Maybe every prophet needs a shrink, and every shrink, a prophet. Maybe every relationship needs both, just as every person needs both shrink and prophet—to ground us and inspire our movement; to counsel patience and encourage us; to hold us back and push us forward; to wait with us at the water's edge to assess the dangers and to invite us to swim with confidence.*
>
> *The prophet sees through the lens of the future.*
>
> *Yes, I have seen us as friends, among the best friends either of us will ever have. . . .*
>
> *The shrink sees through the lens of the past.*
>
> *Memory. Grounding. Integration.*
>
> *This is the work of the present.*
>
> *We cannot be friends at this time.*
>
> *Neither shrink nor prophet hold The Answer or The Truth. Together we are shaping what is true and right for us. This is no power-struggle. It is a mutual becoming.*

Nothing could be clearer to me than the radical mutuality in our relationship. With Elizabeth, I've been learning patience, becoming grounded in the present, able to assess danger and safety, realizing my capacity to swim—and to wait—and this is very good.

If, as I experience Elizabeth, she too has been learning, it is, I am confident, a quality of personal confidence in our power-in-relation, a sacred movement in which professional and personal integrity is in an ongoing process of relational formation—and this is very good.

Yes, we met in the winter of 1987 when each of us was ready (this is kairos, sacred timing)—open, learning, growing already. It was truly as if we were put in each other's paths (I have no doubt that we were), in this moment of mutual readiness, to offer each other gifts each has needed to become more fully herself.

For Elizabeth, the gift, I believe, has been a new (renewed or "becoming") sense of personal confidence, personal courage, to keep moving with our power-in-relation (you, Sophia). . . . For me, the gift has been patience: learning to take time to become rooted and grounded in myself—time to re-member what has been dismembered: the reality of Sophie, for instance, which becomes a key to my seeing the connections between my concerns for justice, my passion for friendship, and my faith in the Sacred—the creative, redemptive Spirit—who comes to us when we are ready in the forms we can recognize and the forms we need.

The relationship with Elizabeth has been, and is, a remarkable occasion of mutual gifting,

a shared blessing.

As my therapist for a while, my sister in the broader panorama of our life together on the earth, and I trust someday as a good friend, Elizabeth's soul has touched mine. In this "touching," she has helped me find patience—and, in slowing down and taking time, I have found my Self—my Source—my Sophie/Sophia—my Soul.

And patience—slowing down, going at my own best rhythm, moving gradually—has enabled me, finally, to remember Sophie's birth

in me as the root and origin of the rest of my life. And everything I believe,
yearn for, value, and am committed to, everything worth living for, is
grounded in this moment, forty years ago, when the Power that creates
and liberates and sustains us all came to me as "Sophie"—a little black
girl—and spoke with confidence:

> *"You need a friend.*
> *So do I.*
> *Here I am."*

> *On this offer, I stake my life—*
> *And it is good.*

In July we had ended, I am confident, in mutual intimacy and
delight. This sense of delight and connection had sparked "The
Friendship Pages." But when I shared them with Elizabeth in August,
assuming I was picking up emotionally where we had left off in July,
she was outraged.

She spoke of my pushiness, my inability to accept her "no,"
my desire to have my "own way," my needing "to be taught a lesson."
"*Never*," she shook with rage, "*never will we be friends. The answer is
no. No. No. Is that clear, Carter?*"

"I don't understand where your rage is coming from." I was
stunned. "I brought you a gift, an offering, in what I was reading.
What have I done, Elizabeth?"

"You know the answer to that question, Carter," came the
angry reply.

Looking back, it's hard for me to imagine how, in this context, I continued to sit in her office—with her, on the floor, separated
only by a candle and a couple of feet—for another hour. But I did.
What's more, we had a fine, upbeat conversation! We discussed the
pictures I'd taken of her in July; the race for the presidency and how, if

it weren't such a racist country, Jesse Jackson would have been running for president. We talked about Maine and old Teraph and Bev's and my other dog, Scudder; about Elizabeth's dog and her own imminent departure for vacation at her place in the woods of northern New York State.

In the middle of the conversation, I asked, "When's your birthday?"

"September . . . " She smiled, then frowned and stopped short. Instant metamorphosis. "Why do you want to know that?" she demanded.

"I don't know." I felt my face flush with embarrassment. "I guess I just like to know when folks' birthdays are so I can think of them."

"Well, I don't give out that information in here," she snapped.

I felt slapped.

"How do you feel about *that?*" she asked, as if she were mocking me emotionally.

"Angry, trivialized, and beaten up."

"That's too bad, Carter. You're manipulative. You want your own way. You usually get what you want, don't you?"

"No, I don't. I feel like you don't even know me when you talk like this. You're not talking about me, and I believe you know this."

"Well, you won't get what you want in *this* relationship. Is that clear to you? You're going to be taught a lesson."

"Elizabeth, why do you want to hurt me?"

"You're responsible for whatever hurt you're feeling right now," she replied.

I felt myself shaking. My gut was queasy. I felt as if I were going to throw up. I wanted to cry, but couldn't. Instead, I spoke.

"Elizabeth, you're so afraid. Why? What is scaring you so?"

"I'm *not* afraid!" she protested.

From early in the therapy, Elizabeth had hinted that she suspected I needed to look at my relationship with my mother.

In this moment, I told Elizabeth she reminded me of my mother.

"How?"

"I experience you both as frightened women," I said, "scared of your passion, your own most creative energy—and you have so much."

Elizabeth was expressionless.

I thought also of how unalike they were. Never for an instant had I known my mother to be cruel, but rather an immensely generous, sweet-spirited woman, anxious about being a powerful woman, and in this sense, a compliant daughter of patriarchy, an incarnation of its logic. Even so, I had always experienced Mama as a woman of tenacious kindness and of a loving openness to the new, spiritually and politically, privately and publicly. Here and now, by contrast, I was experiencing Elizabeth's cruelty and closed-mindedness as a testimony to the same patriarchal logic: like my mother, and like me, she obviously had been educated by life and profession to be frightened of our sacred power. Terrified of Sophia.

"You're both magnificent women who obviously feel deeply and are wonderfully intelligent," I said. "But the world has taught you *fear*—of yourself, your passion, and now of me and my passion. You wanted me to stay in therapy long enough to deal with my mother? Well, that seems to be exactly what I've done, doesn't it? Stayed long enough to see clearly that good, strong women like my mother, and you, and me, teach each other to be terrified of ourselves in our passion."

Elizabeth looked stunned.

"That's a lesson Mama taught me, despite being a marvelous woman and mother in most ways. And you've replicated it, Elizabeth.

I guess I needed to learn this: that strong, passionate women and girls are as likely to be disempowered by women as by men in hetero/sexist patriarchy."

Elizabeth was staring at me.

"My mother and I continue to struggle through this with each other, and that's very wonderful." I thought of the many talks my mother and I had had over the last fifteen or twenty years, in which she and I had dipped deeply together into our feelings about ourselves, one another, and the world. I was aware of what a remarkable, courageous woman Mama was—and, I sensed, Elizabeth, too. "I wish you and I could continue struggling, as sisters together in the world. We could help each other learn how not to do this to other women. We can only learn it together. I need to learn it too, Elizabeth. We all do."

Elizabeth's face reflected a sadness and resignation that come with a sense of having failed. She said nothing.

I LEFT THE August session in a state of emotional shock and immense sadness, but I knew, at last, that therapy had to end.

I had agreed to meet with Elizabeth once more, in September, to say good-bye. The final session was dreadful. Still hoping against hope, I'd wished it could be something other than awful, but the wounds were too deep. I was trying to be as much myself as possible—honest about my feelings and my experience of us as sisters, and still "pushy," wishing we could find ways to sustain an ongoing relationship, willing to go away for months or years, but hoping that someday she would change her mind as she once had said she might.

She spoke angrily: "I only said that because I didn't want to hurt your feelings." The words fell like stones in my soul.

"Either you're lying right now or this whole therapeutic process has been a sham," I responded. "And I have to believe you're lying right now."

Elizabeth's eyes were pained.

A few moments passed. Then I spoke: "How I wish we could simply *talk* about friendship and why these conversations have been so emotionally loaded for us. I wish we could just spend a little time talking honestly to each other about what this has been like for *both* of us. I wish you could talk to me honestly, Elizabeth."

"The problem with that, Carter, is that if we were to have such a conversation, we'd already be friends."

"And what would be the matter with that?" I asked.

"It would mean you'd have won. You'd have gotten your way, and I cannot let that happen."

I shook my head. I didn't cry. I was angry and clear: "God, this has turned into a horribly abusive relationship. But that's not all it's been. It also has restored me to life, and I'm deeply grateful to you for that."

Elizabeth was silent.

"How do you *feel* about me?" I asked. "Now that we're ending, I'd like to know how you really *feel* about me."

"I think you're very courageous."

"But how do you *feel?*"

She said nothing.

"I've grown to love you as a sister, Elizabeth, and this ending is breaking my heart."

She was silent.

I reached into my bag and retrieved two farewell gifts for her: a priest's stole, representing what I had learned in new ways with her—that our power is sacred only insofar as it is shared; and a small limestone bird an old Nicaraguan woman had handed me in 1984, telling me that "love is stronger than fear."

Elizabeth smiled, thanked me, and sat silently with me for a minute or so.

Getting ready to leave, I gathered up my belongings and got up. She stood up with me. We moved toward each other and, as we had done frequently at the end of our sessions, we embraced. This time, however, the embrace was not warm or tender; it was stiff and awkward.

Moving away, I said, "I'd rather say *adios*—'go with God'— than good-bye."

She was silent.

"*Adios*, Elizabeth," I said, opening the door to leave.

"*Good-bye*, Carter," she responded, punctuating each syllable, and shutting the door forcefully behind me as I left.

As the door slammed, I felt small and diminished. Sobbing on the way home, I stopped to see my friend Lane.

"I feel so guilty about what I just did, about what I just said to her." I was choking as I spoke.

"You are speaking the words of a battered woman," Lane replied.

"But she *tried* to treat me well," I insisted. "She didn't mean to hurt me this way."

"I am sure she didn't."

PART TWO

Tapestry of Healing

I WOULD BE HEALING from this relational wounding for the rest of my life,
not because Elizabeth's and my relationship was the source of a terrible
violence, because it wasn't. Relative to most wounding, our relationship was small, minor, and difficult even to comprehend as "violent."
But it would become a window, for me, and for my healing companions, into deeper understandings of what strengthens and what diminishes us. I would be healing for the rest of my life not because, in itself,
this one relationship hurt me, though it did, but precisely because my

relationship to Elizabeth was a window through which I would come to see that what happened in our relationship has been happening forever in hetero/sexist patriarchy. It has been happening to all whose passion for intimacy and authenticity, for justice, mutuality, and, in that sense, friendship, has challenged the authority of patriarchal logic.

This part of my book reflects the most intense period of my healing from therapy. It would begin when I left Elizabeth's office for the last time in September 1988 and would continue through the spring of 1991. During this time, I would be immersed in a process that would not erase or, necessarily, ease my pain, but rather would be opening me more to it. I would be learning not so much to fear the pain as to let it teach me.

If I were a visual artist, I would be painting on a large canvas at this point to show you what happened during these next years. Or perhaps Sophie would be weaving a tapestry with images of her profoundly relational movement, her sacred power that not only kept me sane but has opened me more and more to myself, others, and the world. As it is, I have these words with which to "weave." So I invite you to imagine that I am weaving this process of healing as a theological tapestry. In this work, imagine that I am interweaving four colors of thread, each representing a primary healing resource, in the design of *five nonpatriarchal images of sacred power.* Representing the primary healing resources in my life during this period would be forest, olive, and lime green threads for my continuing journey in *recovery* from alcoholism and bulimia. Shades of yellow, gold, and brown would reflect my *vocational commitments* as a teacher, priest, theologian, and political activist. Bright, navy, and slate blue, gray, and silver threads would signify my *primary healing relationships.* Throughout the tapestry, soft lavender and bright purple threads would designate larger and smaller moments of *meditation, prayer, quietness, and journaling.*

Although the tapestry's patterns would emerge gradually, one by one—*voice, mutuality, earthcreature, compassion, ambiguity*—it would become increasingly clear to me that each had always been in the process of being intricately and inextricably interwoven with the others. Each is a dimension of sacred power, and all of them together are its very essence, the source of all that is creative and liberating.

The rest of this part of the book will be an attempt to weave with words these patterns of God as they emerged in my life over a two-and-a-half-year period, bringing me more fully into friendship with Sophia as they increasingly were freeing me from vestiges of psychospiritual bondage to patriarchal logic.

> *i heard you in Nicaragua and in the wind*
> *i saw you in therapy and in the colony of ants crawling over the*
> > *rock on Little Rye[1]*
> *i walked among your small daisies at Neuengamme*
> *i touch your breasts with my tongue sometimes when you are*
> > *sleeping*
> *i watch you in Robert and Isabel and grieve for you in*
> > *Teraph[2]*
> *i meet you in my classes and wrestle with you in this poetry*
> *i love your linking our lives, wrapping us together as a gift to*
> > *one another.*

——— FIRST PATTERN: *Voice*

I KNEW THAT Elizabeth and I had a creative, caring connection that had been distorted. I knew there was something wrong with a system of treatment that notices greater potential for harm than healing in authentic relationship between healers and those who seek their help and that fails to notice as *harmful* those rules and boundaries that block authenticity. I did not know why I was in such horrendous pain. In the days and weeks immediately following the end of therapy, I thought I was going mad. I was in tears much of the time. Often I would awake sobbing in the morning.

Throughout this period, I was involved in the Twelve-Step program, with its origins in Alcoholics Anonymous. As in good friendship, the force for healing in AA is the power generated among people who are sharing the truths of our lives out of an experience of mutual vulnerability and hope. By *vulnerability*, I mean *openness*—to joy and sorrow; suffering and healing; contrition, amends making, and a willingness to be forgiven and to forgive where there has been injury and where there genuinely is repentance. In the Boston area, New York City, and Maine, I already had found circles of healing companions through a common commitment to recovery.

Week by week, sometimes more often, I went to meetings. In the fall of 1988, it was more to listen than to speak. This in part was because my regular meeting was filled with people in therapy and psychotherapists, at least one of whom, I knew, was a friend of Elizabeth's. It didn't feel right to me at the time even to allude to my situation in a context in which others of Elizabeth's colleagues and clients might recognize the person about whom I was speaking.

I knew of course that the way to recover from addiction is not to focus on what someone else has done to us but rather on what we have done to ourselves through the misuse of alcohol or other substances. I was trying, a day at a time, to be attentive to myself; trying to accept the fact that, regardless of what Elizabeth had said or done to me, and regardless of how much pain I was in, it would only get worse if I began to drink again or if I tried to numb the pain through nicotine or large quantities of food. And so I went to meetings, my regular weekly meeting and others, as a way of letting others help me stay with my pain rather than stuff it.

I found I didn't have to articulate the details of what had happened in order to communicate that I had experienced an immensely painful "relational rupture." This term signaled my experience of an authentic bond that had been broken, a love that had been disrupted, rather than a crazy-making connection or a wrong-relation that should never have happened in the first place. Naming the crisis a "relational rupture" rather than simply a "bad therapy experience" was a way of trusting my own perceptions.

MOST MORNINGS, after crying, I would light a candle and sit for ten or fifteen minutes before taking Teraph and Scudder out for their morning romp around Fresh Pond reservoir. I often would write poems, prayers—whatever would come. Sometimes I would draw from my "angel cards" (a little resource for prayer and meditation) a word and picture to help me focus, intellectually at least, on the possibility of some inner peace. I might, for instance, draw "joy" or "clarity." I would sit with this word, imagining what it would be like to be feeling joy rather than on the verge of tears in most waking moments, or what it would be like to be clear about what had happened and why, rather than so confused. What had I done to contribute to this break? Had it been my impatience? my pushiness? Had I been manipulative, trying to have my own way? What would I learn if I were to sit quietly, not drink, not overeat, walk with the dogs, go to meetings? Every morning, every noon, every evening, I would pray: "God, grant me the serenity to accept the things I cannot change, courage to change the things I can, and wisdom to know the difference." Wisdom to know the difference. Wisdom. Sophia. I felt like a little girl clinging to a strong friend, Sophie.

There was a recurrent dream: I am flying through the air, at peace, when suddenly I crash into a mountain I have not seen, and the small wooden box that I am carrying is smashed to smithereens. The wood splinters in my hand, and I see the contents falling with me toward the earth. I realize I've been badly hurt, but I'm more concerned with saving the feather and the small stone, Teraph's puppy collar and my AA medallion, as they float along beside me than I am with my own wounds.

In waking life, this box and its contents are precious to me. They represent a serenity, a peace of mind, that has eluded me in my adult years but which, in sobriety, I am beginning to realize. The dream suggests to me that the rupture with Elizabeth had uprooted the seedling of serenity I had begun to cultivate earlier in therapy, with her help.

Soon after the termination of my therapy, Jan Surrey had commented that I was manifesting symptoms often associated with a post-traumatic stress disorder—a condition, often following an experience of sudden or severe violence, in which a person suffers nightmares, flashbacks, insomnia, crying spells, and so forth. I was becoming aware that psychologically and physically I was suffering the effects of violence. Along with the seemingly incessant crying, my hair turned entirely gray within four months of the therapy's ending.

In the winter of 1988, while I was still in therapy, Jan and I had begun to meet regularly. She was teaching me to meditate, to sit with the Spirit, to take the time I seldom had seemed to have simply to *be* with a sister, becoming aware in the moment of the power with us, ours in mutual relation. Jan had believed with me that this was, in fact, the power Elizabeth and I had tapped together, much as it was the same power that had brought Bev and me together many years earlier and had sustained us, even through hard places of addiction, places of disconnection from one another.

Jan was immensely sad about Elizabeth's and my disconnection. As a psychologist she was deeply troubled about the implications of what had transpired for her own work as a therapist and as a woman attempting, with her Stone Center colleagues, to generate constructive theoretical work that might enable therapists to work in more mutually empowering ways with one another and their clients.

I was beginning to realize, within a couple of weeks of the termination of therapy, that I wanted to find ways of incorporating lessons from this experience into my own professional work and that I needed to do this if my theological reflections on mutual relation were to continue to have integrity—that is, if they were to continue being grounded in actual relational experiences, including my own, rather than being theoretically abstract and idealized.

Jan and I already had set the stage for such a shared professional endeavor by having planned to offer a course at the Episcopal Divinity School in the fall of 1988 on mutuality. It was too soon for me to speak publicly in detail of the pain or the power-dynamics between Elizabeth and me. But I could begin to speak, in a general way, of the damage that can be done through any relationship—including a professional healing relationship—in which possibilities for mutual authenticity and empowerment are not allowed.

I also began to share with a number of my students a little of what had happened and to let them know that I needed to learn and teach from the pain of this experience. In several cases, students found my sharing disquieting and troubling and did not know how to respond to me. At the same time, there were students whose educational efforts were clarified, sharpened, and moved along, in creative directions, at least in part by experiencing my vulnerability. Was I right or wrong to be sharing in this way? Were these the bad boundaries Elizabeth had been worried about? Or was it a means of cultivating fertile relational soil for theological and educational harvesting? Was it in some way both?

At the time, I was clear that I literally could not work at all unless I was free to explore, theologically, ethically, and pastorally, what had happened between Elizabeth and me. I also believed that my collegial partnership with Jan in the context of this professional exploration, together with my work in recovery through the Twelve-Step program and my most intimate relationships, would help me bring my pain into the classroom without exploiting my students. I knew that I was not seeking from them an agreement with, or acquiescence to, my perspective, nor would anyone be punished for responding to me either negatively or not at all. I simply could not teach a theology of mutual relation without letting those who were studying mutuality with me know that I had been devastated by an experience of mutual relation being undermined by fear and by basic tenets of the mental-health and healing professions that many seminarians come to study and to appropriate for their own work as counselors, priests, and pastors.

DURING MY THERAPY, Elizabeth had referred Bev and me to Cass for couples therapy, and we had been working with her since the fall of 1987. Though we met with her erratically, about once a month whenever Bev was visiting me in Massachusetts, our sessions with Cass had given us an important laboratory within which to test our newly developing communication skills. Here we were, women in our mid forties and fifties, a theologian and an ethicist both widely published on issues of mutuality, justice, and women's well-being, who were beginning to realize the extent to which our own capacities for mutuality had been impeded by social and personal wounds and by an addictive use of alcohol to numb the pain.

Our love for each other was beyond questioning. So, too, was our strong desire to continue reconstructing our relationship as sisters and friends, colleagues and lovers. We were together in recovery from addiction as well as in a commitment to do what we could on behalf of justice. All along, a shared political commitment to liberation, linked closely with theology, had been for Bev and me a foundation of our relationship. In this context, my bond with Elizabeth, and the enormity of my pain in its rupture, had puzzled Bev. It also had hurt her.

She knew without my saying so that I had been in love with Elizabeth, and she had suspected that something similar had been happening for Elizabeth. Given our own relational difficulties—our inability to let the other know what we needed or wanted emotionally—Bev was not surprised that I would have been drawn to someone by whom I was feeling heard and who, perhaps, was allowing me to spark her own emotional yearnings. This was a hurtful realization for Bev, and for me in relation to her, but it did not surprise either of us. It only signaled to us both that we needed to keep working on our relationship.

What did surprise Bev was my being so horribly crushed by Elizabeth's refusal to become my friend. Bev interpreted this clearly as Elizabeth's problem and was puzzled, as she said, by why I had even wanted to become a friend of a therapist who had serious misgivings about becoming friends with former clients.

"What interests you in such a person?" Bev had asked over lunch one day in Maine in August 1988. "This is hardly the sort of person you're attracted to!"

I had told Bev that I really loved Elizabeth, uptight as she was. "She's a sister, Bev. She and I have something to do *together,* something beyond therapy."

Later, one evening in the fall, as I was grieving the ruptured relationship, Bev said again how puzzled she was that I cared so much about such a rigid, hurtful woman.

"Bev, I loved her. I still do. Not as someone I want to be lovers with, though I have erotic feelings. But mainly, I love her as a sister. I mean, literally, a sister. I have incredible grief that she has thrown me out of her life. I can't explain it." Tears rolled down my face.

"I look forward to the day, my love, when you will experience a deep anger at Elizabeth, because there was no good excuse for her to cut you off the way she did. No professional tradition can ethically justify her behavior. As far as I'm concerned, this was an abusive relationship, and I am furious at Elizabeth Farro." Bev spoke sharply.

"I know you are. And I love your advocacy of me! But you didn't know Elizabeth and you don't realize how much she helped me claim my power, professionally, theologically, otherwise. You also don't know how deeply she was yearning to be opened more fully to her own power, which she was coming into through our relationship." I felt defensive of Elizabeth.

"I'm sure you're right, Carter. I know that you wouldn't have valued her if what you're saying weren't true. You don't fantasize relationships! I know that about you. I'm sure that, if I were to get to know this woman, I'd find the truth in what you're saying, but I must say again that there can be no good excuse for her refusal to work this thing through with you. Whether or not she ever wanted to be your friend was beside the point. The central professional issue in this was Elizabeth's failure to respond to your pain. You were in great distress, being profoundly hurt, and you needed help with this—if not from her, then from someone else. It was her responsibility to see this and respond to it."

"You're right. She could have had a third person meet with us to help us hear each other," I suggested.

"You bet. Elizabeth should have seen that some sort of an intervention was needed by both of you, to help you hear each other. But if she wasn't able to admit to you or anyone else, and probably not even to herself, that *she* was in trouble, at least she could have proposed that someone be brought in to help *you*."

"I once asked her if she'd let Jan or Jean Miller or one of the other Stone Center associates come into one of our sessions and help us think through this thing about friendship."

"And she said no, right?"

"Yeah. That's what she said."

Often a bearer of Sophia, Bev shook her head and sighed.

O Sophia! the only folks who could drive me crazier than these
bittersweet angels with whom i wrestle are the women who dare to imag-
ine that each of us, separately and by herself, can create her own destiny,
and that this is enough. it is neither true nor enough!

give me my visions and values, my angels and demons, my music
and marches, my lovers and friends, my comrades and healers, even my
madness, and let us wrestle one another toward the re-creation of a world
in which no one is hungry, abused, destitute, alone—no one, not one of
us. only that will be enough

Early in this healing period, about a month after Elizabeth's
and my termination, I took a three-week leave of absence from my
seminary teaching in order to make a private retreat. This was a period
in which I literally could not stop crying. I spent most of October 1988
with Teraph, Scudder, and two of our cats, Rubyfruit and Samdino, in
Bev's and my small house in Maine. As a means of recording what I
had been learning *theologically* through the therapy and its aftermath, I
spent these weeks writing much of *Touching Our Strength: The Erotic*
as Power and the Love of God.[3] The writing was clarifying, at moments
thea-phonic: an occasion in which the sacred Spirit was manifesting
Herself.

The primary therapeutic significance of this intense period of
writing was that, through it, I was finding my voice as a lesbian feminist theologian of liberation. Yes, I had been badly hurt, and I was only
at the beginning of understanding much of what had happened, but
already I knew the sacred—creative, liberating—character of the power
Elizabeth and I had shared before we lost it to a fear generated by ages
upon ages of violence.

Writing *Touching Our Strength* was my way of witnessing to "the erotic as power and the love of God," a power and a love that I had known from the beginning among family, friends, and creatures of many species but that I had not been able to hold or bear gratefully in my soul. It seemed to me that Elizabeth and I had been holding this power up to the bright light of the morning sun to inspect it carefully together. *Touching Our Strength* was a description of what we had seen and was, for the record, a testimony to the fact that we had seen it. It was the best way I could find of laying claim to my own experience.

I was writing in defiance of the relational rupture and as a challenge to us both and to all sisters and brothers, friends and lovers who have experienced, even fleetingly, the erotic as sacred power. "Don't give up now!" was a message I intended to convey to Elizabeth, to myself, and to anyone who might read the book in a spirit of openness to possibilities of healing from relational wounds and of liberation from oppression.

SAMDINO, MY REMARKABLE white-and-black Manx cat, sat in my lap day in and day out as I wrote. Several times, from the beginning of Elizabeth's and my relationship, Samdino had seemed to me to be bringing me "messages" from Elizabeth. This feels like a strange confession to be making here, in the pages of a book. I had never before heard animals "talk." But then, I had never before seen ladies in the lupine.

Perhaps it was the extent of my grief? Maybe I was, to some degree, out of my mind? Surely I was out of my *rational* mind, and that was fine with me. I cannot explain Samdino or tell you exactly what he "told" me, only that Elizabeth and I were indeed sisters, connected and real to each other. "Don't give up now!" was a message Samdino was conveying to me—from Elizabeth? from Sophie, the Sophia voices I was hearing?

My crying did not cease throughout the fall. If anything, it intensified, but in my soul as well as my intellect I realized that whatever had transpired in therapy, and whatever was happening now, in its aftermath, was being moved along by an erotic, creative, justice-seeking, and compassionate spirit. Maybe I *was* going crazy? Planted in my soul was a seed of faith that, if I was going mad, it was happening at the heart of God. I was afraid, but I was also open and expectant. Physically, I trembled a lot and at times would hear myself stuttering.

When we've tried so hard to love one another, wrestled toward a way of being mutual and safe, struggled and failed, we can rest assured that you are moving us along in ways we cannot know or control.
you tell me our love will not be wasted.

For over a year, Susan DeMattos and I had been meeting once a month in Cambridge's Pentimento restaurant, a gathering place for folks, mainly women, to meet, eat, and talk without rushing. Susan and I went back to the early 1970s at Union Theological Seminary in New York, where we had first met. We had been interested in ministry as priests in the Episcopal church, though the ordained Episcopal ministry was, at the time, closed to women. Our professional paths had diverged over the years, Susan becoming a substance-abuse counselor and I a priest. Both of us had been "out" lesbians for a long time by the time we reconnected in 1986 to discuss how to intervene in a mutual friend's active alcoholism. In the spring of 1987, we had begun meeting regularly to discuss our lives, work, faith journeys, relationships, sexuality—everything connected to everything else. I loved and admired Susan's lesbian, feminist, razor-sharp mind and the depth of her compassion for lesbian sisters.

Late in 1987, five or six months into my therapy, Susan and I had learned that we both were seeing Elizabeth as clients. Elizabeth had not been happy that we had discovered this in one of our conversations, and we had acquiesced to her request that we not discuss our respective therapies with each other. And so, until a month or two after the termination of my therapy, I had not told Susan anything about what had transpired between Elizabeth and me, other than the fact that we had ended. When, late in the fall of 1988, I did tell Susan what had happened, and found myself weeping in the restaurant, Susan took my hands, held them tightly, and thanked me for being a "good sister" to her, for being honest and, thereby, opening up what Adrienne Rich has called "possibilities of truth between us, the possibility of life between us."[4]

IN MASSACHUSETTS AND New York I was continuing to write my book. I was teaching my classes at the seminary. I talked almost daily with Jan, my spiritual soulmate. I meditated regularly. Took long walks with Teraph and Scudder. Spent every other weekend with Bev, resting together, playing, testing ways of communicating, seeing Cass, and going to Twelve-Step meetings. And every morning and noon-time and evening I prayed, again, for the serenity to accept the things I could not change; courage to change the things I could; and wisdom to know the difference.

Still, in the morning, I would be crying. When would the pain end? Or would it?

Over Bev's protests ("I don't want you to continue making yourself vulnerable to Elizabeth," she said), I had written Elizabeth several notes, every three to four weeks, beginning two weeks after our termination. The theme in each was the same: "I ask you to meet me as a sister, to explore with me what has happened between us. I am in great pain, and I suspect you are too."

There had been no reply.

In November, Martha Alsup and Susan Galvin, two lesbian therapists from the Boston area, were murdered while vacationing in the Caribbean. Reading about this horrible event, I sent Elizabeth a card telling her that, in the wake of these murders, I wanted to reach out to her, as a sister who missed and loved her. Again, I asked her to meet me, as a peer, to look at what had happened.

There was no response.

Finishing final revisions of *Touching Our Strength* in December, I wrote her again to tell her about the book and to say that, unless she instructed me not to, I would be dedicating it to her, using only her initials, since she had been instrumental in helping me "touch our strength." "The book, in many ways, is written to you," I noted.

you've been teaching me for almost half a century, but i'm just getting it. i'm beginning to see that the difference between the patriarchal kingdom of god and your sacred realm is that, in the former, a symbolic universe is ordered carefully to hold the power in place, whereas, with you, a symbol is useful only insofar as it helps us become real.

with you, symbols are important. they can be life-enhancing, critical to our well-being. we participate through them, in bearing power with and for one another—as healers, teachers, sacramentalists, advocates, parents, and servants in our professional and personal relations.

in your realm, however, a symbol is not a means of holding on to power, but of giving it up. sharing power, we become real together. no longer in symbolic relation, we become friends.

open our eyes that we may see.

─────── SECOND PATTERN: *Mutuality*

IN JANUARY 1989 Bev and I spent three weeks in Maine. Taking this time and space away to be with each other, our animals, and our women friends in the Deer Isle area was a gift to our relationship. During this little break, I was able to talk more about my pain and the relationship with Elizabeth than I had previously done with Bev. I felt ashamed of having been so emotionally bound up with Elizabeth at a depth that I had not acknowledged fully to Bev or really even to myself. Although Elizabeth and I had not been sexual lovers, *I had experienced us as emotional lovers and spiritual sojourners.* The significance of this for me was just beginning to unfold.

Every Friday night Bev and I would go to the Deer Isle women's meeting at the town hall and enter into a situation of shared vulnerability with other women, including several of our good friends. In this small Twelve-Step meeting, I felt able to speak more freely of the therapy rupture than in either Boston (where I feared people might know Elizabeth) or New York (where I found the meetings too big for much intimate sharing).

"I have been struggling to stay sane, not to drink or overeat, and it's really hard in the wake of this relational break. I am in such pain." I told the women about the murders of the therapists in the Caribbean. I said this had sparked my awareness that it had mattered a great deal to me that both Elizabeth and I were *lesbians.* I explained that her rejection of a friendship with me had been especially difficult for me to understand or accept in the context of a world in which we lesbians *need* one another's sisterly solidarity. "It would not have been as devastating to me if she weren't a lesbian," I declared.

After the meeting, several of us hung around to talk.

"You'd have kicked the jerk in the balls if a male therapist had treated you this way!" Tina laughed.

"I wouldn't have ever gotten myself into this situation with a male therapist, or a straight female therapist either, who was as uptight as Elizabeth," I added.

"So what's keeping you so codependent?" asked Charlotte, gingerly and gently. Here was a splendid sister, employing a language I find misleading because it so lacks a critical power-analysis and, for that reason, suggests that our relational wounds stem largely from our "diseased" selves and "dysfunctional" families.

Still, Charlotte is a gutsy, caring woman with lots of insight. Her question struck me as important, and I heard her willingness to ask it as a gesture of love.

"I don't know. I'm in such pain." I felt the tears well up. "I feel like the pain will never end."

"It will, my dear," another of the women, Laura, assured me with a hug. "You were emotionally battered by Elizabeth and you loved her. You still do. You're beginning a long journey home from an experience of being used like an emotional yo-yo by someone who invited you to help her be open to you, pushed you away each time you tried, and had the audacity to punish you for being pushy!" Laura was an old college friend who had heard me to speech repeatedly during the past year as I had begun to talk with my friends about my therapy.

"Just keep talking about it," Laura continued. "You need to do this, and the rest of us need to learn with you about it. It's all about what we women do to each other. Who needs men to inflict the wounds?—though that's where it begins for us all in this sexist society, I'm convinced."

"This pain feels to me like it's steeped in generations of violence against us," I added. "It feels like its *larger* than Elizabeth's and my relationship, and larger than anything that's ever happened to me personally. I feel like I'm drowning in it."

"Well, sweetheart, you won't, not unless you pick up a drink." Tina spoke confidently. "And if you do that, you will."

you sat with me when we were young and taught me to cut through the niceties. please, Sophie, teach me again.

you say i must trust you. i say, what do you mean?

you say, remember the mustard seed. i ask, is your voice often so small, so hidden, so easy to miss?

you say, yes, often. i say i don't know if i can hear that well.

you say that's why i can't rely solely on myself, it's why i must learn to hear with those whose lives i trust if i wish you to teach me.

When Bev and I arrived back in Cambridge in late January, a letter from Elizabeth was waiting. In it, she wrote that I seemed to imagine that there was some possibility that we could yet be friends. She noted that we had agreed that our work together had been good and that it had ended. She said that this was the last time she would attempt to make clear to me that we would not be friends. Furthermore, she wrote, since she was not open to relating to me as a friend, colleague, patient, or former patient, she did not want me to dedicate *Touching Our Strength* to her (in the end, I didn't).[5] Finally, she asked me not to contact her again and sent me her best wishes. She addressed me in the letter as "Carter" and signed it Elizabeth P. Farro, M.D. This seemed to underscore that, from her perspective, ours had been strictly a professional relationship and that any notion I had of it becoming something other than that was simply in my own confused mind. It read like a letter that, if necessary, could become a part of a legal defense in a malpractice suit.

I was crushed. What hurt me was not so much her negative response but the coldness and deadness of the feeling in it. Had I only *imagined* that this was a person who genuinely cared about me? *Had* I fabricated the bond between us? *Was* it all in my mind?

Bev read the letter immediately. "Well, she is making it clear, Carter. She is a rigid woman who will not be moved. 'To hell with your feelings,' she's telling you. For her to be open in any way to you would be, in her own mind, for you to gain power over her."

"She's unable to imagine anything mutual between us," I agreed. "I'm either beneath her or above her. There is no possibility of our sharing power."

"Right. That's what you do with friends, and Elizabeth's telling you that you will remain beneath her. Period."

"Bev, she's telling me I really don't exist anymore for her as a real person, a sister, someone she has loved."

"No, Carter, to the contrary. This god-awful, tight-ass letter tells me that Elizabeth Farro has to keep you as far away from her as possible. Otherwise, her whole life would unravel."

I CALLED JAN to share the letter with her. She was silent as I finished reading.

"Oh, Carter, I am so sorry this is happening. She seems so frightened and so angry. I feel such sadness." Jan paused. "How are *you?*"

"Really hurting. In a lot of pain." I paused. "I'm wondering if maybe I should go back into therapy, God help me!"

"No," Jan responded. "I think you don't need to do that. You need to be doing just what you're doing—using the Twelve-Step program, talking with friends, taking as much time and space and quietness as you can. I'm amazed that you're able to stay with the pain the way you are."

"But, Jan, I think I really do need to talk with someone, specifically about what happened in therapy, and try to find out why I'm in such pain. God knows, I don't ever again, under any circumstance, want to be in a traditional psychotherapy situation, but I would like to have someone besides you and Bev, who are both so close to the situation, help me look at what happened. I'm wondering about Marjorie McClure. Do you know her?"

"I know who she is."

"What do you think of my talking to her about this?"

"How do you know her?"

"She and I had a wonderful conversation last spring after one of the [Stone Center] Colloquia, and I know a woman who's seeing her who thinks the world of her."

"You could ask her. I've heard positive things about her work. I really don't think you need to be in therapy, but maybe just a few sessions would be helpful."

I'd been very moved by what one of Marjorie McClure's clients, Fran, a student of mine, had told me about Marjorie's response to her upon the death of Fran's child. I decided to call Marjorie and ask if she would see me professionally—as Jan had suggested, possibly only for several meetings—to help me understand the enormity of the pain I was feeling, especially after receiving Elizabeth's letter.

I phoned her and briefly explained my situation.

"I really don't understand the depth and ongoingness of the pain I'm in," I said.

"It sounds like you've been through an ordeal. I'm very sorry this has happened to you," Marjorie responded. "It shouldn't have."

I began to choke up. "Would you be willing to see me for a while?"

"I have an alternative suggestion. Given what has happened to you, I don't think you need to be back in a formal therapeutic situation. I think you might need someone to talk it through with, and I'd be glad to help with this. As a clinician, I need help with the issues you're raising. I think you can probably help me as much as I can you. What if we were to meet every other week for several months, alternately at your home and mine, and just talk together, as two women?"

I was weeping at my end of the phone.

"Carter?"

"Yes," I managed to say, "that would be great. I'd like that." I continued to cry.

"Can you share with me what you're experiencing right now?"

I could say nothing for a moment. Then I spoke. "As you were talking, I realized that this is what I had needed all along, with Elizabeth. *It's what I meant by friendship.*"

"That's what I thought."

So Marjorie and I met six times, three times in Cambridge, three times on the South Shore. In this context, I told her as much as I could about my experience of Elizabeth's and my relationship.

Why had I cared so much about Elizabeth? she asked me. What had this bond really meant to me, and, it seemed to me, to Elizabeth? I was able to tell Marjorie, and to hear myself saying, that from the first phone call I had made to Elizabeth, I had intuited a strong, uncommon connection between us. And I believed that Elizabeth had, too. Elizabeth and I were about the same age; she was a little older. Both of us were professional women, "out" lesbians in our work, having suffered—each in our own ways, I am sure, but also, I imagined, in some similar ways. We seemed to *know* each other deeply, and both of us had indicated an excitement and joy in this relationship. I had known there was some transference going on, but I had believed that there was more to it than that. Had we fallen in love with each other? I thought so, but it was other and more than that. It had seemed to me that Elizabeth and I were on a *spiritual pilgrimage* together, one that we *had* to make, *both* of us. Through my own professional life, I had learned to trust feelings of being in love for what they can teach us about ourselves, one another, the world, and that which is sacred. I had been frightened by these feelings in relation to Elizabeth, but I had been determined to study them and let them teach me. Elizabeth had seemed to me terrified of this dynamic. She had not said this, but her terror at times had seemed to me to fill the room.

There had not been anything inappropriate about the relationship, I said. But in order for it to have remained a creative and empowering connection, it could not have remained indefinitely a traditionally structured psychotherapeutic relationship. Marjorie agreed with this. From the outset, I had intuited that the relationship either would grow and change, or would hurt me badly. Marjorie pointed out that this might well have been why I was so adamant about friendship.

My work with Marjorie was clarifying: I was *not* crazy. I had *not* fabricated a mutuality that had never existed. I had *not* experienced simply a serious "transference neurosis," though Marjorie pointed out that this is exactly how it would be understood and treated within the malestream of psychiatry in which both she and Elizabeth had been educated.

Marjorie helped me see that, while it is certainly possible, and can be quite splendid, for therapists and former clients to become friends, Elizabeth's professional training would have discouraged—maybe, in her own mind, even prohibited—any movement in this direction. Marjorie gave me a view of psychiatric practice from the therapist's perspective, allowing me to see to some degree what had happened through Elizabeth's eyes.

"Carter, I suspect she would have needed a stronger, more supportive circle of colleagues to have been able to take the risks of letting the relationship change. We therapists tend to practice too much in isolation or only with a supervisor who normally counsels caution. I believe that her cutting off of this relationship had nothing to do with her lack of caring for you. It's just that she didn't know how to move forward, and she probably felt very alone and scared. Certainly, the letter she wrote you suggests to me that her *own* experience of the relationship is very frightening to her."

Marjorie's and my meetings every other week ended when Bev and I left again to spend the summer of 1989 in Maine. My pain was beginning to ease. I was becoming a little more patient with the healing process because I was beginning to realize how truly others in my life—my students, Marjorie, Jan, Bev, other friends—were on this healing journey with me and that we were, in ways none of us knew fully, moving with one another along the path of liberation.

> *and why, Sophia,*
> *did i need*
> *assurance*
> *the relationship*
> *would not*

simply end
once the
therapy
was done?
because i knew
so well that
the spiritual
basis of our
work was
the power
we were tapping
through the
mutuality of
what was
happening
between us.
and i knew
that simply
to end, to
say goodbye
and walk away,
would break
your sacred
heart,
and it did.

A year earlier, in the spring of 1988, Jan and her colleague Jean Baker Miller had invited me to make a presentation as part of the Stone Center Colloquium series. In March 1989, I delivered a lecture, "Coming Out and Relational Empowerment: A Lesbian Feminist Theological Perspective," to an audience largely of women mental-health professionals.[6] In this paper I was able to make some connections between my understanding of the politics of lesbianism, especially of living openly as lesbian women, and a deeply human yearning for mutual relation, for sisterliness and brotherliness, in all areas of our lives, including the psychotherapy relationship. Later in the spring, I spoke before a gathering of psychotherapists in New York City who meet annually to explore clinical connections between addiction and homophobia.[7] With this group also, I raised questions about traditional medical and psychoanalytic/psychodynamic models of treatment for lesbian or gay addicts like myself, or for any sister or brother engaged in the work of healing and liberation that we all need and together can find ways of sharing.

In neither lecture did I discuss, or even mention, my own therapy experience. This was not because I feared that to do so would detract from the "objectivity" of my perspective. With many feminist and liberation analysts, I understand genuine objectivity to be *radically honest co-subjectivity,* in which we are clear and up-front about our biases and experiences and are working together with one another, as co-subjects, toward fuller understandings of what may be more nearly "objectively" true.[8]

I did not mention my therapy experience because I was not prepared at the time, emotionally or intellectually, to meet the resistance I feared my story would evoke among psychotherapists. I could be "out" as a lesbian and an alcoholic. I was beginning to be "out" as a bulimarexic woman. I was coming out in these papers in the spring of 1989 as a friendly critic of the traditional psychotherapeutic structure. But I was still not ready to be "out" as a woman who had longed to sustain a mutually empowering relationship with a therapist whom she had loved, and who had been rejected. I expected that most psychotherapists would attempt to explain to me how unprofessional or unethical Elizabeth would have been to meet me as a friend and how, therefore, what had happened had been, finally, in my best interests as well as hers.

I was not prepared, emotionally, to be so patronized, and I was not ready, intellectually or emotionally, in the spring of 1989, to join publicly an argument about professional ethics. This would come later. For now, I knew that neither psychotherapists, nor priests, nor pastors, nor teachers, nor anyone else should treat those who seek their help as I had been treated. I knew that no patient, client, or student should be so badly hurt in relation to those to whom they have turned for help. And I knew that what had transpired between Elizabeth and me was, at root, *systemic:* it was about the structures of our public, professional, and personal lives, and about healing the wounded and liberating the oppressed in a patriarchal social order founded on dynamics of nonmutual, fear-based, control.

These two public lectures in the spring of 1989 gave me an opportunity to begin deconstructing the dynamics of control that form the social basis of patriarchy *at its best.*

BEFORE LEAVING FOR Maine, I wrote Elizabeth a letter. Though she had asked me not to contact her again, I was hoping that time, and my own sense of connectedness, would enable her to open a little toward me. I told her of my work with Marjorie McClure and invited her, again (as I would every eight, ten, or twelve months into the future), to meet me, as a sister, to explore together what had happened, perhaps with a third person to help us, someone we could choose together. Before mailing the letter, I asked Barbara Harris, my good friend and bishop, to bless the letter and to bless me as its sender and Elizabeth as its receiver.

"May God strengthen you both and keep you open to all possibilities for healing, reconciliation, and forgiveness," Barbara prayed as she stood with me, a hand on my shoulder.

BACK IN MAINE for the summer of 1989, I continued to go to meetings, take long walks with Teraph and Scudder, and be with Bev. I was frequently in touch by phone with Jan and regularly with a handful of good women friends on the island. I was reading in feminist liberation theology, ethics, and theory in preparation for teaching and several professional commitments I had made for the coming year. I also was sleeping a lot, resting, journaling, praying, and meditating.

I was thrilled that the summer would be extending into a sabbatical, for which I had few plans other than to remain on Deer Isle until hunting season began in November. As much as I was enjoying the summer, I was looking forward to a time of solitude, which, except for a few days on an island during an Outward Bound excursion in 1988, I had never experienced.

stopping the drinking, the smoking, the bingeing and purging, has enabled me to slow down and notice your presence which has been with me all along. in this rebirth of consciousness, i am in touch again with you. i am learning to trust you and am astonished to see that you trust me too and that you lust after me as a lover.

for my sisters on Deer Isle

During the first year of healing from therapy, my friends helped me realize that being gentle with myself was essential to the process that was unfolding and teaching me what I could not yet see. *Moreover, I had begun to see that every person helping me struggle through my pain was someone also being healed with me through this struggle.*

Renae, for example, is a friend in Cambridge who had been sexually abused by a prominent male psychoanalyst in Boston. She had been his patient for seven years in her teens and early twenties, and he had had sex with her regularly during her visits in his office. I knew nothing about this when I met Renae in 1987 through the Twelve-Step program in the Boston area. We would get together only occasionally, always with much to share. During one of our conversations in the fall of 1988, still not knowing about her experience in analysis, I had told Renae about Elizabeth and me. She had been deeply empathic and sorrowful, especially since she knew Elizabeth casually and liked her.

Almost a year later, as the summer of 1989 drew to a close, I received a call from Renae:

"Just checking in," she said. "And I want to share something with you." She proceeded to say that, after I had told her about my therapy experience and she had seen the pain in me, she felt as if she had entered my pain and couldn't get out of it. "I could not forget how I felt when you told me," she said. "My feelings obviously were about something other than *your* experience."

Renae told me that, gradually during the next months, she had realized that what had happened to her in relation to her analyst had been, in fact, abusive. She had never forgotten the experience (it had been twenty-five years earlier), but until I shared my pain with her, she had not felt that her own pain was valid, she said.

"I want to thank you for helping me realize my own pain, Carter. I couldn't have done it if you hadn't shared yours."

Months earlier, Marjorie McClure had suggested to me that Elizabeth probably was attempting to avoid even the possibility of sexually abusing a patient. I had realized this. How ironic, Renae and I agreed, that it would be specifically Elizabeth's treatment and the pain it generated in me that would spark Renae's awareness of her own pain at the hands of a sexually abusive psychiatrist.

The connection made by Renae sharpened my realization that I had been *abused*—not sexually, but emotionally. It was becoming increasingly clear to me that abuse—damage, harm, violence—can result from a professional's refusal to be authentically present with those who seek help; and that such abuse can be triggered as surely by the drawing of boundaries too tightly as by a failure to draw them at all.

o how i yearned to bless my healer, to share comfort and courage, delight and respect.

i wanted to sit with her, to touch her hands and meet her heart, not so much as the priest i am as the sister i was becoming with her.

how i yearned to bless her, to walk beside her as a friend, but she seemed not to care, not to hear, not to see it was the sweetest, gentlest spirit she was crushing.

o, Sophia, i was so wounded in my soul, and you gathered me up and held me with tender affirmation.

you put the twinkle back in my eye, mended the crack in my heart, and poured it full of your compassion.

———— THIRD PATTERN: *Earthcreature*

SABBATICAL HAD BEGUN. I was there in the cottage with Teraph, Scudder, Samdino, Rubyfruit, and Bev's very special kitty, Neffertiti, Rubyfruit's sister. Anne Gilson and I had rescued Neffy several years earlier from a man who was threatening to kill her because as a short-haired tiger, she was different from the other, long-haired kittens in the litter. Before I had stopped drinking, the idea of spending a day, much less two months, pretty much alone—that is, with the animals, birds, and other creatures and a human friend from time to time—would have terrified me, especially since I had little to *do*. I had committed myself only to writing two brief essays by November for a couple of progressive christian journals on topics that interested me and, in this moment, felt timely: one was on suffering and Christ;[9] the other was on how, as a theologian, my mind had changed during the decade of the 1980s.[10]

On September 15, 1989, exactly one year after I left Elizabeth's office for the last time, I awoke with a poem in mind:

One year later
i bury a
stone and with it
the power of your
fear in my
life.

It was a rainy autumn day. After sitting with a candle and having breakfast, I donned my rain gear, called the dogs, and headed down the gravel country road for our morning romp. On the way home, an hour later, we were met by Samdino, who often would walk with us. I reached down to pat him and wound up picking him up to cuddle him at his insistence and try to dry him off a little—not easy in the pouring rain.

Lifting him to me, I also took a small stone and, with both stone and cat in hand, headed on. Once we were home, Teraph, Scudder, Samdino, and soon Rubyfruit sat around me as I dug a small hole and buried the stone in the yard. I then sat, surrounded by animal companions, for quite some time, my arms and face lifted up, drenched. It was not clear to me what was rain and what was tears.

Was I ready to give up the fear?

DAYS AND NIGHTS would come and go. The moon's phases would change and with them my body-rhythm. September in Maine is possibly the most exquisite month of all. Lots of bright blue sky. Warm air. Cool breeze. Some brilliant leaves, though mainly evergreen on the island. And almost no noise whatsoever in or around the small house, which sits in a meadow on a cove. Stone buried, I was weeping still, but I was no longer afraid that I was going crazy or that the pain would not end. With my friends' help, animals and humans, I had become more patient, gentler with myself and, therefore, probably, with others.

I loved being with our animals, and on some days I would sit with one or the other for hours, stroking him or her, talking and listening.

Do animals talk? Yes, they talk. Do we listen?

THERE ON DEER ISLE in the autumn of 1989, I was experiencing the dynamic wholeness of creation. Whatever assumptions I still took somewhat seriously regarding the pragmatic value of hierarchically ordered, static power arrangements in institutions, society, or creation began to vanish during this period. I began to experience and envision us—not just humans, all of us—as participants in a creative project that requires us to struggle toward living in mutual relation with one another if we are not to be lost to fear and its offsprings, despair and cynicism, hatred and violence. I began more often to experience myself as an "earthcreature," yearning for right-relation with animals and the earth, a relation that most of us white westerners do not know how to embody very well. During this period I began to think that, ethically, we ought not to be raising animals to kill and eat, and that probably we should not be eating animals at all.

My father, Bob, was present with me on Deer Isle that fall. I would find myself talking with him sometimes as I walked. At first, I felt I should be outraged at what he had done to me—the beating that I had remembered with Elizabeth. But I wasn't angry. I was more confused than anything, and incredulous. How could a man so gentle, and so genuinely caring, as Daddy have beaten me like that?

My sister, Ann, my brother, Robbie, and I had tried to remember instances in our lives that would have supported my memory of such a beating, and we could not. We could remember several times when Daddy had disciplined us or lost his temper, but we could not remember any violence or harm done to any of us, or to anyone else, by our father. In fact, we remembered him as an uncommonly compassionate character with the patience of Job. The memory of his violent behavior toward me did not feel accurate. I had not thought much about the two horrible memories since leaving therapy. My pain, it was evident to me and to my closest companions, had more to do with what had transpired between Elizabeth and me than with my memories of what had happened between my father and me or the yardman Jeff and me.

During the fall on Deer Isle, however, I opened the box of materials I had written during therapy and had sealed several weeks after the termination. Inside were bits and pieces of poetry, prayer, letters to Elizabeth, notes following almost every session, pictures I'd drawn, and images and visions that had come to me during the eighteen months of my work with Elizabeth. When I opened the box I recalled one such image:

Several months before I had remembered the beating, my father had appeared to me in a dream. I was in a mental hospital in the dream and did not want Elizabeth Farro to treat me. Something had happened and I didn't trust her. In fact, I was terrified of her. I was in a straitjacket, tied down in a bed, when my father appeared. "I've come to tell you something, Sugar," he said. "Don't be afraid of Dr. Farro. She's her daddy's little girl. She needs you to be patient with her. You'll go through a lot of pain, but you won't be destroyed. You'll be changed. And I'll never be far from you. I'll go with you through whatever happens."

Being reminded of this dream, I was startled and more confused than ever. What on earth could this have to do with the memory of being beaten by the very man who had said he would go with me through the pain?

"Daddy!" I cried, one afternoon, walking alongside Teraph, who, now in his thirteenth year, was hobbling. "I don't understand! What happened to me? Tell me. Speak to me, for God's sake, Daddy!"

The windchill was smacking my face as we paced ourselves slowly across the causeway. My cheeks were cold. Scudder had run ahead of us and was scavenging on the beach a hundred yards away. I stopped, stepped out on the large stones at the side of the road, and sat down among them. A few seconds later I heard Teraph whining and looked around and saw him several feet away, trying to get his uncooperative old canine legs to bring him closer to me. It wasn't going to work, so I got up and stepped back to him. Kneeling in front of him, I rubbed his face and head and legs and began to sob uncontrollably:

"Oh Daddy! Teraph! Sophia! Jesus! I don't know who I'm talking to right now. But please bear with me through this confusion! And for God's sake, Teraph, please don't die yet! It's bad enough that Daddy's gone, and Elizabeth. I need your help, Teraph! Daddy! Sophie! Jesus!—and Scudder!" I laughed and hugged her as she squeezed into my arms. She and Teraph were both licking my face with enthusiasm.

I stood up and turned around to head home, dogs at my side.

I felt as if I had been heard, and I knew that Teraph, Scudder, and I were walking in the presence of a power greater than ourselves.

dear Jesus,

you helped me understand the trauma in having my passion treated as pushy and my pain as a manipulative ploy.

you showed me this is how the church has treated us all along.

you reminded me that this mis-understanding of your power inflicts a wound so deep in the soul that few survive.

you gave me your trembling, bloody hands, as old and bent as God Herself, and invited me to come with you through a pain that felt unbearable.

Every Friday night I would go into town for the women's meeting.

"You're looking rested, Carter!" Charlotte declared one evening. "Being away from the city is doing you good! You look more rested than I've ever seen you."

"Maybe I'm beginning to know a little better how to take care of myself," I replied. "It's also not hard to feel more at peace here on this island, given its place in the lives of us folks 'from away.' For me it's a resting place."

I spoke further about this when the meeting formally began. "I'm just feeling better and better," I affirmed. "And I'm still feeling pain, lots of it. But very little fear anymore. A lot of gratitude. This fall I've been discovering how much at heart I am an *earthcreature* and that this is true of us all. You know, I really believe that that's what recovery is leading us toward—a sense of our commonness and intouchness and mutuality not only with other human sisters and brothers but with all creatures great and small."

UNTIL THE FALL of 1989, I had not lived much in the realm of mystical consciousness. I had always been more interested in justice than enlightenment, more concerned that we live in right-relation here and now than that we turn ourselves over to a spirit who will mend our lives, relationships, and world in some place and time other than this one.[11]

This process of healing, however, was moving me well beyond the dichotomous assumption that it is an *either/or*—that we work for justice in this world *or* open with one another to another, related realm of envisioning. Healing from the wounded/wounding therapy involved for me a shifting of consciousness: I was *not* being drawn away from realizing the material, embodied wrongness of the relationship, but I was being pulled toward experiencing, in its many psychological and political dimensions, my relationship with Elizabeth as part of a larger tapestry of personal trauma and healing, of social violence and liberation—larger than either she or I could possibly have imagined as we labored together, doctor and patient, under the conditions of tightly drawn professional boundaries.

we're like
a potted plant
i said when
she asked why
i wanted us
to end therapy
someday and
be friends.
we'll need more
space and
light and
other plants
with us to
help nourish
us and keep
us growing
and alive.
we'll need to
be put outside
into the
garden where
our roots will
deepen our
colors become
bold and our
stems green
and supple.
you, Sophia, were

inviting us
into more
space, your
space, i
believe.

————— FOURTH PATTERN: *Compassion*

THE SABBATICAL HAD allowed me to experience time more slowly, as a gift, and to move around in space uncluttered with business-as-usual. Even after my animal friends and I left Deer Isle, at the outset of hunting season, and headed to New York City in November 1989 to spend two months with Bev, I was enjoying waking and sleeping more in my body-rhythm; feeling, more keenly than I could recall ever having felt, my own energy level rise and fall; knowing when it was time for sleep, time for walking, time for eating. I felt as if I had begun to be at home with myself, and I spoke of this at times in Twelve-Step meetings.

Though I could still, in a moment, weep over the fracture with Elizabeth, and still did each time I flashed back upon particular moments in the relationship, I had a growing sense of having known this woman well and having loved her. She was not, I think, getting larger than life, idealized, with the passage of time. To the contrary, I was more deeply aware that, through both her caring attentiveness and her cruelty, her capacity for loving and her rejection of me, I had met an authentic character, a real person, Elizabeth—and, in this genuine meeting, I had met myself, not idealized and not diminished, but the real me. Slowly, I was beginning to see us both.

The problem with traditional psychologies is that, like traditional christian theologies, they fail to recognize the radicality of our *co-subjectivity*. Psychologists could study Elizabeth's and my case for years and never come close to understanding what was happening if they persisted in constructing their analysis upon such self-versus-other or ego-based categories as projection and transference. We western white people tend to make far too much of our individualities as the basis and goal of both our health and our moral responsibility. And we make far too little of what Charles Williams called our "co-inherence" and Martin Buber understood to be the basis of an "I-Thou" experience of our life together.[12]

This fundamental epistemological problem—the theological and ethical, psychological and political problem of how we know what we know—had been the basis of my critique, and that of other feminist, Mujerista, and womanist liberation theologians, of white western patriarchal christian theology.[13] It was also the basis of the Stone Center's critique of traditional psychologies and, implicitly, of traditional theories of psychodynamic psychotherapy.[14]

Jan Surrey and I were becoming increasingly fascinated by our professional colleagues', and our own, resistances to exploring the implications of radically relational psychological, theological, and ethical theory for the actual practice of both ministry and psychotherapy. As practitioners ourselves, we realized that changes in practice cannot happen responsibly overnight. But we believed that it was time for women clinicians, clergy, and other practitioners to start exploring together how we might act differently—more mutually, more as co-subjects—in our work.

By the time my sabbatical drew toward an end in December 1989, Jan and I were outlining plans for a workshop on mutuality in psychotherapy.[15] I was also beginning to think about the presentation I would be making through the auspices of the Association of Gay and Lesbian Psychiatrists at the annual meeting of the American Psychiatric Association in May 1990. I had been asked to speak, as a lesbian, on spirituality. I had agreed to focus more specifically on the spirituality and morality of psychotherapy as a social institution and as a relationship.

In the meantime Christmas had come, and the whole Heyward family had arrived in New York to celebrate the christian holy season and the New Year. Day after day, we would go out to see the lights and the city, take the kids and dogs to the park, visit museums, restaurants, and theaters, and sit glued to the TV, watching one Eastern European nation after the other shed its communist shell. The whole bunch of us was ambivalent about what was happening and why. Most of all, we wondered what it would mean not only for Europe but for the rest of the world as well, especially for the vast majority of men, women, children, and other creatures who do not benefit at all from capitalism's global advance.

We were especially concerned about women—about an increase in violence against women of all colors and cultures, about women's reproductive freedoms being whittled away even further; and about Jews, in Germany and elsewhere, and the rise of anti-Semitism. We sensed also that racism was being saluted and, along with sexism and hetero/sexism, promoted by the chain of events happening electronically right before our eyes in Europe late in 1989. All in all, we found the 1989 holiday season unsettling. It seemed to us that, despite the *apparent* victory in Europe of the people over despotic rulers and dysfunctional governments, all was not well. Had the principalities and powers, the unjust rulers of our life together as a global network of flesh and blood, taken the upper hand? What on earth were such words as *democracy* and *freedom* coming to mean? What had they ever meant?

Along with large numbers of United States citizens, mostly white, middle-strata, I had looked to Nicaragua as a small sign of what is possible when people really *do* attempt to build a free and democratic society around the needs of the poor rather than the aspirations of the rich. I discussed this with my loved ones over the New Year celebration. It seemed to me that the upcoming elections in Nicaragua might actually signal a new direction for many of the smaller, poorer nations in the two-thirds world. I felt that there might be more good news for the long run in Nicaragua than, for example, in the newly unified Germany.

Several months earlier I had agreed to join a Witness for Peace delegation to observe the elections in Nicaragua. Twice before, I had been a guest in this Central American country for very short periods. Like many U.S. citizens and other "internationals," I had been powerfully inspired by the Sandinistas' broad-based efforts over decades to liberate the nation from the tyranny of economic and military control and exploitation by the United States and our puppets within Nicaragua.

For eleven years, since the overthrow of the Somoza dynasty by the Sandinistas in 1979, United States forces had been working to overthrow the Sandinistas. Despite this ongoing assault by the *contra* against the poor in Nicaragua—most Nicaraguans—the Sandinistas seemed, to most progressive analysts and activists in Nicaragua and elsewhere, to have succeeded in keeping the nation officially free of U.S. domination. The elections that were to be held on February 25, 1990, were likely, most progressives figured, to vindicate the Sandinistas' revolutionary long-term effort by formally establishing Daniel Ortega as president of Nicaragua and by putting many of his Sandinista comrades into governmental posts throughout the nation.

However, on the morning of February 26, our group of Witness for Peace observers in the small town of Rio Blanco in central eastern Nicaragua awoke to the news that Violetta Chamorro of the U.S.-backed UNO (United Nicaraguan Opposition) coalition had won the presidency by a significant margin. The Sandinistas were officially out and, with them, the vision of a mixed socialist-capitalist economy and of one small American nation able to operate with some independence from the economic and military hegemony of the United States.

We U.S. citizens felt a combination of shame, sorrow, anger, and, finally, astonishment and inspiration as we listened to our Nicaraguan companions, in the wake of the defeat, tell *us* not to lose heart! "The revolution cannot be destroyed," they assured us. "It will continue in the hearts and minds and work and lives of many generations of men and women who love life and, for that reason, will always refuse to worship the forces of death and oppression." They thanked *us* for helping them realize this by coming to stand with them; and, all the while, they were telling us that we needed to go home filled with a hope we had received from them. "Whether we are in Nicaragua or in the United States," one of our Nicaraguan friends said, "we must never forget to look upon the enemies of justice with compassion, because, as Jesus says, they do not realize what they are doing."

I had taken with me on this trip a small journal. In it I had pasted pictures of several with whom, in Spirit, I believed I was going to Nicaragua: Bev. Jan. Teraph and our other animal companions. My mother, Mary Ann. My father, Bob. My sister, Ann, and her husband, Bruce. My nephew, Robert, and my niece, Isabel. My brother, Robbie. And, finally, Elizabeth.

On the flight back, I wrote, next to Elizabeth's picture, "Jesus, my brother, Sophia, my spirit-guide, Teach me compassion." Again, I was weeping, and my good friend and doctoral student Mary comforted me.

Upon my arrival back home, Bev told me that Teraph had barely made it.

"I really thought I'd have to have him put down. He went into such a decline when you were gone. His legs just gave out. I said, 'Teraph, please hang on till Carter gets back!' I couldn't bear the thought of his dying without you."

Teraph, a wolfhound-shepherd-collie combination, weighed about one hundred pounds and, at age thirteen and a half, was way past his life expectancy. I had been preparing for this moment for several years, but nonetheless could not imagine how I would make it through this loss without going crazy. I at times had laughed with Bev, Jan, and others, saying that Teraph was my "longest-standing primary relationship," and this was, in its own special way, true. I had never loved another creature of any species more than Teraph.

Upon my arrival home, Teraph had come back to life, but it became clear to me over the next couple of weeks that he had rallied for *me* and was still in a terrible pain that was written all over his body. I knew that he was holding on for my sake, and that I had to let him go for his.

So, on March 19, a number of friends who had been favorites of Teraph's over the years joined in a farewell party for him. Dr. Heather Weihl, a compassionate veterinarian, had agreed to come to my home so that Teraph could die on his own bed with a minimum of fear. Jan had come over earlier in the day and had meditated with Teraph and me, and Bev of course had come from New York.[16] We ordered a chocolate cake from the incomparable Rosie's Bakery for the occasion, and Teraph ate heartily from it. Everyone had a chance to say good-bye to him, and I, finally, took several minutes alone with Teraph, to bless him and let him go as best I could. When the time came, Heather administered the injections, and after a few final, hard moments of struggling to stay alive, Teraph slipped away in my arms. I had lain beside him to stroke him as he died. Holding his furry body as he went, I found myself remembering that Elizabeth had told me that one of the reasons she would not become a friend was because I did not know how to let go of those whom I love.

I was weeping, thinking how much easier in the soul it is to let go when love is being honored and celebrated than when it is being twisted by fear, lies, and betrayal.

when we betray or batter, lie to or deny, those whom we love, we rip into the heart of God Herself.

the only adequate response, you say, both yours and ours, is a sorrow too deep for words, and a renewed commitment.

Upon my return from Nicaragua, I entered into a short-term therapy relationship with Miriam Greenspan, a friend of Jan's who, she felt, would be a good person with whom to explore further what had happened between Elizabeth and me and why it continued to matter so much to me. Miriam, I understood, believed strongly both in the spiritual basis of all healing and that therapy always has political meanings and consequences. It sounded to me like a good match, Miriam and me, and one that was important and timely, for I had decided before leaving for Nicaragua that I was in enough pain still about the therapy relationship to warrant some specific, focused attention to it when I returned.

As had been true to a lesser degree in my work with Elizabeth, Miriam and I spent much of our time sitting together on the floor, letting come what may out of silence.

What began to emerge in our work was *clarity* about my connection with Elizabeth. Like Miriam and me, I had experienced Elizabeth and me as *sisters* first, doctor and patient second. I had intuited that this had been not only my sense of the relationship, but also Elizabeth's, and I had experienced her *fear*—probably a mixture of strong personal anxiety and professional reinforcement—as an ongoing source of betrayal of our most creative, mutually caring connection.

Miriam had me talk to Elizabeth.

"Tell her what you experienced."

"I experienced your loving me so much that it scared you. I experienced you as too afraid to be honest with me. I experienced you as lying to me through your silence and your words. I experienced your dishonesty as a betrayal of our relationship and your rejection as an act of profound relational contempt."

"Tell her how you feel about that."

"I'm sorry for you, Elizabeth. I'm sorry you were and, I suspect, still are so terrified of me."

"She's terrified of her emotional authenticity, Carter. You evoked it in her. She could have experienced it as a gift and a blessing. Instead, she experienced it as a threat and a danger. But tell her how you really feel about how she treated you."

"I'm furious at you, Elizabeth! I'm outraged that you didn't trust either yourself or me enough to allow us to deal with each other honestly. I'm furious that, in fleeing from the possibility of abusing me, you lied to me, you tossed me back and forth emotionally, and you sealed yourself off forever in a professional container—*not* to protect me from abuse, but yourself from having to be in any way accountable to me. You have a lot of gall to use the language of 'safety' and 'caring' in your practice!"

Miriam was the first person with whom I was able to experience the rage at Elizabeth that Bev had been hoping for a year and a half that I would tap. She was also, in addition to Jan and Bev, a sister with whom I had begun to notice connections between my treatment in therapy and my experience in the church as a lesbian priest whose passion for life, love, and justice the church calls forth—and rejects, again and again, back and forth.

Along with Bev, I had believed truly that anger is an honest, even indispensable, feeling-response to injustice.[17] Until I began to tap the root of my anger at Elizabeth, however, and to see there my anger at the hand that the christian church has dealt passionate women, I had not known the full force of my rage against the misogynist, erotophobic structures put in place historically and held there to this day to keep women under control.

Miriam went with me into this rage and the terrible grief that was accompanying it. She helped me begin to hold these emotions as blessings rather than to fear them. In so doing, she enabled me to begin actually to see and hold Elizabeth—in my emotional stirrings, intellectual reflections, spiritual yearnings, and physical aliveness—as a sister-sojourner who, despite her own longing, was unable to move with me into a new place. Moving into my rage, I began to feel its roots in *love* and *sorrow*—my own and Elizabeth's love, my own and Elizabeth's sorrow. I began to notice that my rage was less at Elizabeth, my sister, and more at the structures of our lives, hers as well as mine—our patriarchal religions, professions, cultures, set in place to impede our mutuality, our co-subjectivity, and our passion as sisters with, and for, one another. Miriam was moving with me into *compassion* with, and for, myself, Elizabeth, Miriam, and all persons whose capacities for intimacy and friendship, trust and mutuality, have been diminished by the coercive demands and violent lessons of hetero/sexist, racist, classist patriarchy.

Miriam helped me see more clearly that Elizabeth's and my relationship was the instrument that most definitively shattered the logic of my having chosen to see a psychiatrist in the first place. As a lesbian feminist christian priest and theologian, I had been tired. Of course I had been tired! But my tiredness was not rooted in an emotional or mental "pathology." Its roots were in the abusive character of a world-church built on the fear and hatred of strong, erotically empowering/empowered women like me. I did not need to be psychologized. I needed to be encouraged to tap the roots of our sacred power. I did not need to be "treated." I needed to be joined by a sister. But the patriarchal logic of my psychospirituality had been enough intact in 1987 to prevent my knowing what I needed, which was exhausting me still further. At that weary point, ironically, I had turned to Elizabeth for help, hoping she would meet me as a sister but unable, at the time, to know this or name it.

I knew from having read Miriam's path-breaking book on women and therapy that what had transpired between Elizabeth and me would not be repeated between us.[18] I knew that for Miriam a therapeutic relationship is an occasion for authentic connection and engagement that can move over time into friendship if the persons are drawn in this direction by common interests, commitments, spirituality—whatever. As we began our work together, Miriam had suggested that one of the primary reasons I needed to work with her was to experience therapy with "a different ending."

Late in the spring of 1990, about four months after we began, Miriam and I ended our professional relationship. Over time, we would be building a relationship of deep and mutual trust, affection, and admiration. We would continue to learn with, and from, one another much about our lives and work, our politics and spiritualities, as a Jewish feminist therapist and author, and a lesbian feminist christian theologian and teacher, with much to give to and much to receive from one another; each a stronger, more compassionate character because of the other.

In the late spring, as I was ending therapy with Miriam, I mentioned to her that I had begun to doubt that the "memories" of the terrible violence in my life were, in fact, actually about my own life. At about this same time, I said over dinner one night to Jan, Bev, and one of my feminist colleagues at the seminary, Demaris Wehr, that I did not believe that these "memories" of being orally raped and badly beaten were memories of my life. To my astonishment, like Miriam, none of these women seemed in the least surprised by this suggestion.

"There's always seemed to me to be something not quite right about these memories," Bev responded. "Something hasn't rung true for me. I have to say that I really don't think you were ever raped or severely beaten, and I've known you for a long time."

Jan seemed pensive, as she often does. "I don't know what to say, except that I trust your intuition and also sense some wisdom in what Bev is saying."

"You know, Carter, I wouldn't be at all surprised if, through your relationship with Elizabeth, you were tapping into *someone else's* experiences of violence. I really do believe that can happen," Demaris mused.

"Not necessarily *someone's* experience," Jan added. "Possibly a larger experience of violence against women, an experience that Elizabeth's treatment moved you into."

Bev was listening intently. "You *do* have a mystical consciousness, Carter! It's one of the things about you I least understand, but I love it!"

The next day, I phoned Demaris, who teaches courses in mysticism and healing, and asked if she'd be willing to meet with me to discuss this further. She said she not only would be willing to meet but would love to get together and wondered how I would feel about our exploring particular relationships in each of our lives that had been both wounding and, possibly, sources of "transpersonal" connection.

Demaris said she wanted to ask my assistance in exploring a question that pertained to her own experience in a healing relationship: how does such a relationship pull the "healee," emotionally and spiritually, into the healer's experience? Not that she and I had experienced anything that *literally* had happened to our respective healers, she said. Rather, she wondered, had we been immersed emotionally and spiritually in the relational *dynamics* that historically had shaped the consciousnesses and commitments of the women to whom we had turned for help? With these sisters, Demaris wondered, might we have passed unawares, in different ways, into a world of violence, woundedness, denial, and power-over—dynamics we experienced through our healers?

Demaris and I would spend eighteen months, from late spring of 1990 through the fall of 1991, probing this possibility. It was apparent to us that our experiences were not uncommon: many women and some men have been badly hurt through therapeutic and other healing relationships. We wanted both to continue the personal healing we each had begun and to consider the *spiritual* dimension of what had happened. We were especially intrigued by the possibility that, through our bonds with Elizabeth and Julie (Demaris's healer), we had entered into experiences, or effects, of violence and brokenness that were not, primarily if at all, connected to the autobiographical details of our own lives as individuals.

Somehow, for me, this strange possibility had become at least imaginable in the aftermath of my sabbatical experience with my animal companions and my father; the trip to Nicaragua with its spiritual implications for the ongoing construction of a global network of compassion; and my recent experiences of both Teraph's death and Miriam's work, which, each in its own way, had opened me more fully to the possibility of the compassion to which our Nicaraguan *compañeros/ compañeras,* and my father, had beckoned me. Bev's abiding faith in my sanity and Jan's own sense of mystical possibilities further encouraged me to go forward in this mutual exploration with Demaris.

Over the next months, meeting a couple of times each summer and weekly during the fall of 1990 and winter/spring of 1990–91, Demaris and I were drawn repeatedly to the prominent role of *fear* in our healers' work and to its by-product, an *emotional dishonesty* with us, which we experienced, increasingly, as emotionally and spiritually abusive. We had been unable to break out of these relationships for reasons both negative (we were "hooked," believing they could help us *and* that they needed us to "save" them) and positive (we genuinely loved them and wanted to work through the relational impasse with them as sisters and friends). Unable to break free, we increasingly had experienced reality—ourselves, our healers, and the world itself— through the lens of our healers' experiences of reality.

In my case, it was as if I had entered a realm of violence through a door provided for me by Elizabeth's perception of the world. With Demaris's help, I began to realize that my visceral, first-person "re-membering" of abuse at the hands of violent men had been brought on simultaneously by the genuine love and healing power between Elizabeth and me, which had rooted and grounded my capacity to see what is what, and by its antithesis, the fear and violent power that had come crashing into the relationship to wound us both, pushing my vision beyond the boundaries of my own life into a larger realm of experience. I had indeed experienced being almost destroyed, sexually and physically. I had been traumatized by both of these horribly violent acts, and nearly killed, it seemed to me. I had been immersed, over a few months, in a deep and terrifying well of violence against a girlchild.

With Demaris, I realized more clearly that patriarchal logic tells us that when we remember something, it is *of course* because, *as individuals*, we saw, heard, or otherwise experienced it. There is no place in the realm of patriarchal logic for transpersonal memory. But I began to see that what I had remembered was not in fact my own autobiographical material.

How can I be sure? I *can't* be 100 percent positive, empirically certain, beyond all doubt, but I am as sure that these events were not mine, personally, as an individual girlchild, as I am sure that I have not been president of the United States in a former life.

I am as sure that these things did not happen to me as a child as I am sure that my dog Teraph died in my arms, in my home, in March 1990, and not somewhere else at some other time.

What then was I learning with Demaris and other friends with whom I was studying this matter?

I was learning that I actually was immersed in the violence that is done to women, girls, boys, and marginalized men, all over the world, during every minute of every day. By *actually*, I mean that what I experienced really happened to someone or some ones, somewhere, at some time. It was not a lie, not a falsehood, not a fiction that I concocted and entered for a while. It was an actual life experience of a person, or persons, being raped and beaten. But who? Elizabeth? My mother? My sister? One of my grandmothers? One of my students or intimate friends? Someone(s) I didn't know personally? I do not know. What I *do* know is that during the spring of 1988, I became a victim not because, as an individual person, I have lived these terrible events, at least not yet. *I became a victim because, as a sister earthcreature, I was being drawn into experiencing as my own the effects of violence and brokenness in the world.* Jan Surrey says that, through compassion, our pain can be a link to the pain of others. I believe that this is what was beginning to happen in my life in the spring of 1988. My pain was beginning to open me to a larger realm of suffering.

I had no idea during therapy that the dynamic between Elizabeth and me triggered this phenomenon, but I believe this is, in fact, what happened. From the beginning of our work together, Elizabeth and I had shared deep spiritual yearnings for, and intimations of, mutuality with one another and elsewhere in our lives. In the summer of 1987, this spark of mutuality had enabled me to begin actually to embody Sophie—our power in mutual relation—as the source of all that is good in the world and in my life. Then, in the fall and winter of 1987–88, a profound psychospiritual dissonance had been created in me between *love* and *fear,* forces raging not simply between Elizabeth and me, but within me. From the moment in January 1988 that I had begun interpreting my pain through Elizabeth's therapeutic lens, fear and self-distrust had taken the upper hand. During the spring, this fear of friendship and passion, a fear of the creative life force itself, had lured me away from Sophia, source of all that is most loving and just. The fear had pulled me into a psychospiritual experience of its own violent essence. *In effect, I was immersed mystically in the violence and abuse that result from our fear of our own most sacred relational power.*

> *i was learning that*
> *we, christic*
> *sisters, have*
> *been shattered*

by the
sins of the
world far
beyond our
capacities
to see or
know.

Healers need to be aware that, in our health, we are always more than simply individual selves. Because this is so, the ways we treat each other not only can generate memories from our own pasts; through our love and our fear, we can catapult one another into realms of experience far beyond the so-called boundaries of our lives as individuals.

And so it was that, in relation to Elizabeth, I remembered violence against women, children, and men who have experienced sexual, physical, emotional, and spiritual violence. Through the therapy, I entered a domain of psychospiritual dissonance in which, emotionally and spiritually, I was shattered, assaulted as truly as if I had been raped and beaten as a child and had split into pieces in order to survive. Through the therapy, I learned more than I had known before about the terror, pain, and unmitigated horror of abuse—childhood sexual and physical violence.

Looking back, I am aware that even in the earliest months of therapy, as soon as Elizabeth announced that we would not be friends, I began to have feelings and intuitions of having been violated. Not surprisingly, Elizabeth and I both would assume that these psychological rumblings were pertaining in some way to my own past. In fact, as early as May 1987, nine months before the memories actually began, the disconnection in the therapy relationship was beginning to throttle my sensibilities and move me toward a trauma that would be larger than my own. This is what I believe was happening.

Something about *us,* something *particular* in Elizabeth's and my relationship, had begun, almost from the beginning of therapy, to move me into an experience of violence. Something about *my* experience of our connection, and, I believe, something about *Elizabeth's* experience as well, had been creating the conditions for this re-membering, because the relational dynamics of healing are never one-way. *Only Elizabeth and I, as sister-sojourners, could have come to understand fully what was happening—to me and to her—and how our experiences were forming one another's.* No professional rules or theory could have moved us through this passage safely. Only a mutual authenticity could have provided a safe passage for us both, and this was not to be.

IN MY MAY 1990 presentation at the American Psychiatric Association's annual meeting in New York, I began to speak publicly of Elizabeth's and my relationship. I hoped to stir compassionate interest among those working in mental health as well as to raise, from a client's perspective, some critical questions about traditional structures of psychological treatment.[19] Many of the psychiatrists did not understand my lecture, like it, and/or find it helpful. Some, however, did and wished to continue the conversation. One was Peggy Hanley-Hackenbruck, a clinician in private practice in Oregon and at the time president of the Association of Gay and Lesbian Psychiatrists. Peggy and I began a correspondence, at first pertaining to professional issues raised for her by my talk and to theological/ethical issues raised for me by her response.

A year later, in the spring of 1991, while I was in Oregon to lecture at Lewis and Clark College, Peggy and I would spend a couple of days birding in the Columbia River gorge, walking through a Japanese garden in Portland, and sharing our senses of having experienced more than our own experience at least once in our lives—in my case, in relation to Elizabeth; in Peggy's, with a former lover.

"You really loved her, didn't you?" Peggy asked.

"Yes."

She paused for a moment, then reflected. "I think it's important to respect and honor my clients, which includes learning from them in ways that stretch me personally."

"Which says to me you're open to growing and changing with them," I added.

"Growing and changing with them is essential to good therapy, but it's not something I was taught." Then she added, "I want to tell you how touched·I am by your love for Elizabeth and by your compassion."

> *i was asking*
> *that someday she quit*
> *being the shrink*
> *she'd been trained*
> *to be and be*
> *my friend*
> *instead,*
> *and she said*
> *she wanted*
> *to say YES*
> *but had to*
> *say NO*
> *and i said*
> *i wanted to*
> *STAY but*
> *had to GO,*
> *and after months*
> *of fierce*
> *struggle, sometimes*
> *cruel and*

crazymaking,
more often tender,
respectful,
i said
FAREWELL
and she said
GOODBYE
and shut
the door.

for the next
two years,
i awoke
each day
feeling as if
my gut were
being sliced
open and i were
choking to death
on pain.

pain?

she had
heard me
to speech,
while i had
called her
forth
and come with her
into our

sacred power
to heal one
another
from the pain.

it was
the most
devastating
relationship
of my life
because, from
the beginning,
it contained
such terrible
repudiation
of its own
most sacred power,
which is yours
to heal the pain.

Holy One, from
the beginning
you were
urging us
to help each
other down
from the god-
damned cross
of these
ill-conceived
death-dealing

distortions of
what is REAL
and GOOD,
of what is
POSSIBLE,
and what is not,
of what
HARMS and
what HEALS.

GENTLY, you
warned, NOT SO
ROUGH, but
it was not
to be an easy
passage.

i believe
neither of us
knew at the
time what
was happening
between us,
and we did
the best
we could.

for days
months years,
i thought i'd die
being ripped

down, torn off
the meathook
of the dispassionate
logic on which
we'd been hung
to rot,
with you.

now down
at last, i hear
you asking
me to quit
being the priest
i'm trained
to be and be
your friend
instead,
and i want
to say YES
and i do say
YES and i
say to you,
BY YOUR POWER,
and you say
to me,
WITH YOUR HELP,
and i lift
my head and
draw deeply
from your
breath to

hold the
pain with
my beloved
sister,
and i do.[20]

———— FIFTH PATTERN: *Ambiguity*

DURING THE PREVIOUS year, I had decided to take a trip to Australia in January of 1991 to visit David, a man with whom, twenty-three years earlier, I had been very much in love. I needed to see him, both because he had been ill and because his and my relationship had been very much like Elizabeth's and mine in several ways: he and Elizabeth both were talented, caring people who had met me primarily, it had seemed to me, as brother/sister-sojourners in processes of profound *spiritual* transformation at moments in our lives when each of us was especially vulnerable to change. In both relationships, I had experienced my love for the other as truly mutual and, in both instances, had wound up feeling as if I had conjured up the relationship in my mind. Both situations had left me feeling crazy, experiencing my reality as simultaneously affirmed and denied.

"I hope David will be able to tell me what was going on with him when we were together in the sixties," I said to Jan. "Like with Elizabeth, it was so bittersweet, so complex, and painful."

"Such ambiguity," Jan was musing. "And we're so horribly equipped through education, professions, and religion to deal with it."

"Right," I continued. "All the 'both/and's—love *and* fear, affirmation *and* denial." I was coming to believe that the capacity to live in ambiguity, to accept it, to make ethical decisions in it and act on these decisions—rather than using ambiguity as an excuse for not taking stands—is a capacity born of wisdom and seasoned in courage.

"We wind up defining life and health according to whatever is *least* ambiguous," Jan reflected, "least open, least chaotic, least threatening . . ."

". . . and most *dead,*" I laughed. "I'll have to say that my relationships with both David and Elizabeth were, as Elizabeth suggested, chaotic, embodying the sort of psychospiritual raw material out of which real love is born, but not without struggle. For Elizabeth, this meant, primarily, danger; for me, it meant a powerfully creative relational opportunity—dangerous, but important."

Even at age twenty-two, with David, I had known intuitively that he and I were a wonderfully creative combination. But it was also true that the major social structures in our lives—such as marriage and the professional forms of christian ministry—couldn't have "contained" David's and my chaos any more than traditional psychotherapy could "contain" Elizabeth's and my relationship. It was not that any of us was bad, or sick, or wrong. It's just that, in our most creative, deeply mutual possibilities, we become dangerous people. We always do—dangerous to the professional and personal structures of patriarchy itself, dangerous to the structures of our own lives. People cannot live this way without strong relational networks of support and solidarity. Neither David and I, nor Elizabeth and I, had such networks. Few people do in capitalist patriarchy. We need to be spinning webs of honest, intimate friendship and support, expanding circles of companions with whom to touch our strength, as a first priority throughout our lives. These God-bearing wombs of compassion are what will enable us to tolerate ambiguity and learn to sift chaos as lightly as a bakerwoman does her flour.

FOR ABOUT A YEAR, David had been recovering from a heart attack and had been taking stock of his life. He wanted to see me, he wrote. I had wanted to see him, too—this lovely man and faithful priest whose vision of justice could (almost) move mountains. Within the first forty-eight hours, we had the first of several immensely important conversations in which we spoke of our relationship, of what had been going on between us in the late 1960s. And so, after more than two decades, I learned that I had not concocted a fantasy of David's having loved me.

I sat quietly with him, trying to absorb the impact of what he was telling me. I felt as if I would cry.

"I loved you, David," I said. "And I still do. I always will. The form of our relationship is not what I would have chosen twenty-three years ago, but I'm here now to celebrate it with you."

We held each other a minute or more, both of us in tears.

"God bless you, Carter," he said, pressing my head against his shoulder.

"And you, too, David!"

Spontaneously, we began to laugh together.

"We would have been quite a pair, wouldn't we have?" he chuckled.

"It probably would have been *wonderful* and *terrible!*" I laughed. "You know, you're a damn good priest!"

"Well, look at you!" he rejoined.

I DID NOT KNOW until I was with David in Melbourne and, several days later, with Sister Angela at the Community of St. Clare, near Sydney, that I would learn more than I could have imagined.

The war in the Persian Gulf began while I was there. In this context, I found myself, with David, Githa (David's aunt), Angela, my brother, Robbie (who had accompanied me), and several Australian women friends—Diane, Gail, and Patricia—in a process of recovering more fully the power to forgive, a power that, for me, had much to do with my healing from therapy and the wounds of patriarchal logic. We were tapping this sacred power not only, or even primarily, as individuals who, in various ways, have wounded one another, though we are that. We are also members of races, nations, and churches that generate fear and wrong-relation, distorting our bodyselves, psyches, politics, spiritualities, and relationships. Social characters, all of us, we often seem to be constructed more in the image of fear than of love. These were issues we were discussing in Australia, concluding that we are both—*lovers* and *afraid.*

Speaking of these things, we talked candidly of brokenness, our own and that of the world. We lifted up the past and the present/future, our politics and spirituality, the abuses and healing in our lives, the structures of oppression and our parts in liberation. We prayed together and sat together. We had celebrated a Eucharist for justice and peace at David's church the night before the war began, and we continued to share vocational visions and commitments of how we ourselves could be involved in the work of liberation.

Through it all, I was aware of a palpable presence of sacred power among us. It was the power to resist violence and heal wounds—large, systemic brokenness, and smaller, personal abuse; old injuries and recent ones as well. As in Nicaragua a year earlier, I had taken Elizabeth's picture with me, along with those of other loved ones. When, occasionally, I would glance at it, I felt sadness and tenderness toward her. Through friendship and prayer, political awareness and meditation, I was being touched and strengthened in my soul by the power to forgive those who inflict wounds and are genuinely repentant. I was being moved also by the power to repent, turn around, make amends, and ask forgiveness of those whose lives I or my people have violated and damaged, those with whom I would wish to stand in solidarity.

Three days before the United States began its evil assault on the people of Iraq, Angela and I sat together at the Monastery of St. Clare in Stroud, New South Wales, and spoke of the impending violence. We reflected on how it was shaping our senses of vocation and accountability to particular groups of people in our nations, churches, and cultural situations. We spoke also of the fear that we and our feminist companions generate among most churchmen and of how well and poorly we cope with the consequences of working closely alongside folks who are frightened of what we represent.

I had been delighted at last to meet this fiery, spirited nun whose face burns with a sacred passion. I had seen her in a film on the struggle for women's ordination in the Anglican church of Australia and had recalled her exclamation in the wake of temporary defeat: "We must *laugh* in the face of the tiger!" she'd roared.

"I've come," I told Angela, "to laugh with you in the face of the tiger!" And that is exactly what we did together in January, laughed and wept and spoke at length from our hearts.[21]

WEEKS LATER, Angela would write me of the immense passion—creative energy—she had experienced between us.

"We are God bearers to one another, Carter! That's what this energy between us is all about. It's such a powerful force for good in the world!"

"Yes," I wrote back, "in you, my beloved friend, I am met by the love of God. You are an incarnation of Sophia to me. Thank you for sitting with me. For helping me pray."

"O darling!" Angela would write later, "your belief in the sacred, erotic character of all creative relationships is such a gift to me. Isn't it *marvelous* how She sends us whomever we need to give us courage and strength to believe in ourselves?" These words coming from a brilliant sculptor who was hearing me more and more to sacred speech.

ANGELA, AS MUCH as anyone in my life, was helping me feel, deeply in my bodyself, erotic power as *sacred* power, the love of God indeed! She and I had not been sexual lovers, just as Elizabeth and I had not been. But the same power was moving with us, between us, around us, and within us—the same creative energy I had experienced with David and Bev, with Jan and Miriam, with Demaris and Peggy, with so many students and teachers and companions, women and men. This is the life the church would beat out of us! Angela and I had spoken this truth together. This is the passion for which we have been nailed historically.

When lesbian therapists say that *they,* unlike other therapists, cannot be intimate with lesbian clients or former clients because the dangers of sexual-boundary violation are too real, do they not see that *all* life-giving relationships are infused with both erotic power and danger? This is not basically a matter of sexual identity because the boundaries of how we experience ourselves sexually are stretched by erotic power. My relationships with Jan, Marjorie McClure, Miriam Greenspan, and Angela have been no less "dangerous" than Elizabeth's and mine—each holding power that is erotic, creative, and sacred, and each "dangerous" in that it threatens to transform us and the ways we work and love.

In relation to those who genuinely love us, what leads us to imagine that our safety is in having no connection at all rather than in struggling fiercely together for right connection?

The most lasting and compassionate revolutions of our women's lives, and of our time, will be won by those who have opted for the danger of struggling for right-relation rather than for the safety of separation from sisters who they fear might love them either too much or not at all.

And why is this a revolutionary option? Because struggling for right, mutually empowering connection does, in itself, empower us together, with one another, to live daring lives on the basis of a strength we have touched together. And our shared strength makes us shapers of history as well as of our own lives as sisters.

ON THE FLIGHT home, Robbie and I talked about what this trip had meant to us. Both of us were angry and sorrowful about the war and our own white middle-strata complicity in it. We wondered what awaited us back in the United States. What resistance would we be joining or helping to shape? We also spoke of our respective relational lives and processes of healing, growth, and change.

"I hope the reunion with David helped ease the lingering pain in your relationship with Elizabeth Farro." Robbie offered the words tenderly and squeezed my hand.

"I think so." I squeezed back affectionately. "Though I'll always feel some sorrow, because I experience her every day as a sister who has cut herself off from me. It's as if she's in an emotional coma, and this grieves me. But the trip has moved me more toward accepting her love and her estrangement as equally real and present and ongoing. David and Angela both were Godsends to me in this way: they helped me see this. They helped me accept the ambiguity."

ABOUT SIX WEEKS later, in March, Angela and I decided, by mail, to "exchange burdens"—a mystical healing tradition. She would carry with me the ongoingness of my sadness in relation to Elizabeth, and I would bear with her the sorrow of rejection, trivialization, and contempt by a church that heaps abuse on strong women. In our own lives, each was no stranger to the other's particular burden, so we could help carry it with a wisdom accrued through experience. Not long afterward, on Easter Sunday, I wrote a prayer with Angela and Elizabeth in mind. In that moment, sitting on a rock in the small cove near our home on Deer Isle, I knew I was ready to move toward completing this book. The emotional burden had become for me a spiritual passage.

you have given me a way of seeing what is invisible to the eye: i see that my pain, and theirs, and that of our sisters and brothers, is yours.

i saw them and loved them. i'd known their pain for a long time, perhaps from the beginning. and when, at last, we met, i saw it immediately, though at first i couldn't trust seeing and knowing them, myself, the world, and you, my love.

we suffer together not because we lack "good boundaries" but because we are sisters.

and you showed me the only way suffering can be redemptive: when our pain is a link to the pain of others, you say, it is our primary resource for compassion and healing; the raw material of solidarity and liberation; the basis of your holy realm both with us now and always coming.

we suffer with one another when we love, and in this godding, you say, the stone is rolled away, and we find ourselves standing at the exit of a tomb that is empty, for we are risen!

for Angela and Elizabeth
Easter Day 1991

PART THREE

Some Ongoing Issues

RELATIONAL POWER AND VIOLATION

I HOPE IT IS by now clear that this was not a case of a "good" woman versus a "bad" one, an "abuser" versus a "victim," one guilty, the other innocent. Both of us were complex characters, deeply human/creaturely, asking the other to be with us, to meet us, in ways we could embody. We were mixtures of innocence and guilt, victimization and our own capacities to abuse. Neither of us meant to wound the other, to misuse power. And there were varieties of power at work between us.

It is not true that Elizabeth had "the power" in our relationship. In the context of psychotherapy, Elizabeth had the *institutional* power to help me heal and to hurt me, and she did both. In the same professional situation, I had a power of *consciousness*, a power of knowing that we both were being drawn into our sacred *relational* power. In ways that I do not know fully, my power both inspired and terrified, and perhaps also healed and harmed, Elizabeth.

I was an intense, emotionally demanding patient who unwittingly overwhelmed her doctor. The positive side of my tenacity has always been a creative, visionary energy and a willingness to risk on behalf of what I value. This was true in my therapy with Elizabeth. On the negative side, I think I often have been difficult for folks whose ways of being emotionally connected are not as intense, not as demanding, not perhaps as potentially "dangerous." I have not always been deeply empathic with, or sensitive to, those whose relational energies are different from my own. I know I was an immensely difficult client for Elizabeth. I know she was frustrated that I couldn't seem to accept her as *she* was in the world—spiritually yearning, but relationally shy and professionally conservative. And she was right: I could not accept her "no" as the final word. I still do not, any more than I accept death as the final passage. But I did then, and do now, *respect* her word because it is *hers*. By *respect* I mean that I took Elizabeth seriously—I heard her. I argued with her. I did not dismiss, trivialize, or reject her.

But I do not imagine that I was a sweet, gentle client who got emotionally screwed by an authoritarian shrink. I experienced us basically as good sisters who tried to be caring and respectful in a relationship that we both valued deeply. That we did not succeed reflects, I believe, our woundedness through the violence that has shaped us all.

violate: TO TRANSGRESS, break, do violence to another.
Can a patient violate a doctor? Yes.

Did I violate Elizabeth? I do not know. I didn't mean to violate her any more than she meant to violate me, and I would like to make amends for whatever hurt or violation I may have inflicted upon her—by pushing so hard against her? or by not pushing hard enough? by failing to leave therapy as soon as I intuited it was not a trustworthy context for my healing? Did I violate Elizabeth by failing to turn my car around on that day in April 1987 and go back to her office and tell her that her rigid posturing on friendship meant that henceforth I could not trust her to help me and therefore that I would not come again? Was my effort to "fix it," to help her be real with me, to make it a trustworthy space, a relational violation? Or was it a way of honest healing for me and potentially for her as well? Was it perhaps both— violating and healing? abusive and loving? And if it was both, what can be learned from this?

The only lessons I am sure of are that we need more compassion in life, which can help us to be patient with one another and ourselves in situations in which efforts genuinely to love may in fact be wounding; and that we need support and encouragement in the relational processes that will teach us compassion. *Elizabeth and I needed support and encouragement from beyond ourselves. For me, the greatest violation by either of us was in our respective failures to insist that we be joined by other women to help us through a situation that was, I believe, shattering us both.*

I have little doubt that Elizabeth also was badly wounded by our relationship. Part of what would have hurt her is that her professional tradition would insist that, as the one responsible for exercising damage control, she failed. This sense of failure is a burden she should not have had to carry. I believe she would not have had to carry it had she allowed others to join in helping us chart a course together that could have been ethically responsible and personally liberating for us both.

What might Elizabeth have said or done differently that would have helped me?

She might have been honest with me all along. Emotionally honest. She might have said that this just wouldn't work as therapy—and why. She might have said that something was happening that was causing her to feel professionally unclear, or insecure, or off base—and told me what, insofar as she could. She might have told me that she just couldn't handle it. Or that she loved me and that this was scaring her. Or that her lover wouldn't stand for the ongoingness of our relationship. Or whatever was, in fact, the case. She might have been honest with me all along, from the outset. And if she couldn't sustain the relationship, either as therapy or friendship, she might have said, "Let's get someone to meet with us to help us end, because, Carter, I don't want you to have to suffer so." I'd have been grieved and sad, but it would have been an altogether different kind of wound—inflicted by love and loss rather than by such an experience of emotional betrayal and relational contempt.

MAKING CONNECTIONS, BUILDING COMMUNITY

Nothing was being affected more significantly in this period of relational crisis than my work as a teacher and priest. All that I was feeling and thinking, speaking and writing, was being permeated with this wounding and healing. A shifting of spiritual, theological, and political foundations in my life had begun in my childhood, with the advent of Sophie and the presence of such people as my high school history teacher, Betty Smith, to call me forth into our sacred power. In my adulthood, I had begun over a decade earlier, in being irregularly ordained and in coming out as a lesbian, to move consciously beyond the boundaries of patriarchal logic.

In the 1970s, with the support of my teachers and companions, I was beginning to speak and write of God as our power in mutual relation.[1] I had hoped that this theological re-imaging would, in some small way, challenge creatively the patriarchal logic of a god/father who needs no friends, but until this therapeutic trauma, I had not known deeply in my soul how surely this power for mutuality topples our lives. I had known that the naming of divine power in a non-hierarchical, immanent way constitutes a breaking rank with the faith of our fathers, but until my relationship with Elizabeth, I had not known how much a daughter of the fathers I had remained, still in need of patriarchal affirmation and definition of my sanity and morality. I had known that the Jesus story continued to be important to me, precisely because he was a brother, not a god, but until the rupture with Elizabeth, I had not realized how hard it is actually to live as sisters, or brothers, in the world.

In my teaching, along with many sisters, I had begun to challenge the patriarchal logic of the world-church long before I entered therapy with Elizabeth. This feminist commitment to professional as well as personal change had been stirred vigorously in response to the dominant ideology and politics of the 1980s. With many, I had lamented a rise in the mean-spiritedness of a society in which violence has been glorified and tenderness condemned, an order fastened in structures of abuse—the exercise of an immutable power-over, which is the quintessence of patriarchal logic—for the benefit of affluent white males and, in a derivative way, for some who aspire to be like them. In this unapologetically oppressive climate, the trips to Nicaragua during the 1980s had become vehicles for my political and theological education. I had been struck there by the evil of the "low-intensity conflict" set in place by the United States. I had been impressed also by the revolutionary faith of many justice-seeking christians, including some marxists. Participation in worship had been for me, in Nicaragua, a way of sharing strength for the struggle against the poverty of mind, body, and soul being perpetrated by my own people.

By the time I entered therapy, I had become more mindful of links between our foreign policy and how our society and psyches are ordered by dynamics of relational control that generate a complex malaise. I was aware that this pervasive social and psychospiritual dis-ease festers both in massive human and creaturely suffering and in the apathy—or nonsuffering—of many who create the conditions for the suffering of others, yet seldom realize what they are doing. For almost a decade I had been attempting to infuse my professional work with these learnings.

I cannot be in a learning arena, whether classroom or psycho-therapy, without wanting *all* participants, if we can, to share and probe *our* experiences as people with particular histories, cultures, and sto-ries; memories, dreams, and commitments. As a *theological* educator in particular, I believed then, as I do now, that we cannot speak intelli-gently about what is sacred unless, together, we are open to hearing what She is saying to and about us; open, that is, to the revelations our daily lives hold for us, the sacred unfolding of our life experiences. In other words, I assumed that every significant meeting—between teacher and student, therapist and client, friend and friend, in groups or as individuals—is an occasion to meet on holy ground and learn to-gether how the Sacred is touching our lives, together and separately, in common and in different ways.

This is the assumption upon which I teach. It was the as-sumption upon which I began, and ended, my therapy. And it was on the basis of this understanding of how we learn what is most impor-tant to our values and visions that my teaching and other professional work was being shaped around the wound incurred through therapy and the processes of healing. This was the only honest context in which I could teach, speak, or write, so pervasive was the pain of my bodyself and soul.

may i move thoughtfully, with the power of your commitment to truth and your passion for justice, among those whom i teach.

may we be for one another living signs of your real presence, your questions, your tenacity and intelligence, your transforming and vulnerable ways of loving this world and all its creatures, including us.

please bear with us and help us keep our humor, our minds, and our courage and, where any of these gifts is lost, teach us how to care for one another as long as we are here together on the earth.

> *for Alison,*
> *whose love transforms,*
> *and for her children.*

What then was I learning on this healing journey about my work as teacher, priest, and counselor? What was I learning in Nicaragua and in the seminary? with Miriam and Bev? with Demaris and Jan? with my students, friends, and animal companions?

I was learning that, as sisters and brothers, we do indeed hear to speech those who come to us. I was learning that we are also called forth by these people, to be more fully ourselves with them. I was learning that this mutual authenticity is the root of all that is genuinely moral, creative, and liberating, whether in teaching, pastoral work, or psychotherapy. I was also learning that this mutually empowering connection does not contravene, or deny, the systemic/institutional power-differential between teachers and students, counselors and clients, doctors and patients.

I was learning that, in our professional work, our good intentions and depth of caring are not enough. I was learning that we who teach, preach, or counsel need to be mindful of the ways in which power is shaped systemically and structurally in our professions.

I was learning not to be self-reliant, not to work alone, but rather to be building networks of supportive colleagues and friends throughout my life and work. I was learning that it is only in such a context of collaboration that we can discover how to hold together, in creative tension, a strong sisterly love and our power-over those who seek our help. We should try to be always in a process of giving this power up responsibly, with the help of our friends and colleagues, letting it be transformed by the power of mutuality.

It had been clear to me all along that Elizabeth had tried to treat me well and fairly; that she meant to be compassionate, empathic, and responsible. It had also become clear to me that, despite her intentions and my own, the relationship became a nightmare for me and, I suspect, for her, too. This situation helped me realize more fully than ever that it is *essential*, not optional, for teachers, pastors, and healers to understand our work systemically and structurally—not simply in terms of personal goals, commitments, and intentions. The most empathic, caring priest in the world can inflict serious harm on those who come for her counsel unless she understands the power she embodies simply because she is an ordained person in a system (institution) that historically has been structured (built, established) by ordained priests *in order to secure their own power,* which, in patriarchal religion/theology, reflects the power of god/father.

For the priest to assume that this is not a problem for her simply because she, personally, doesn't believe such nonsense and doesn't intend to exercise power over others is pastorally inadequate. Such naivete and denial are steeped in a highly individualistic and nonsystemic understanding of power that is professionally irresponsible. On the other hand, for her to accept, as an unchanging absolute, the power she has been ordained to embody is arrogant, unimaginative, patronizing, and serves primarily to secure her good standing as a female patriarch, daughter of god/father.

For a priest, teacher, or therapist either *to refuse to accept her power* or *to refuse to let it be transformed and thereby given up is potentially abusive.* The basic ethical question for healing professionals is how to embody our institutional power in such a way that it is transformed into mutually creative energy between us and those who seek our help. This poses an ethical quandary for all conscientious, creative professionals, which we cannot figure out alone. We need one another's solidarity and presence in discerning how to live, love, and work in more genuinely moral, mutually empowering ways. Only insofar as we are working together on this can we, or the institutions we represent, make significant headway toward liberating those among us who are oppressed or mending that which is broken between and within us.

We should be clear that the problems described in this book are not intrinsic to psychotherapy, as a healing profession, but rather are in the *rigidity* of its interpretation and practice. As with christianity, the trouble lies in the *fundamentalist* assumption that everything must be done as it always has been done on the basis of an unchanging symbolic universe that reflects unchanging power-relations, structures, and rules. This assumption, I believe, lurks near the core of most abusive power-relations, often even those that may appear to reflect too little structure and boundaries that are too loose. Everything creative and liberating in history has originated in our commitments to change the structures, institutions, and conditions of our lives and work. But we cannot make creative or liberating changes working by ourselves. *We need to remember that professional isolation—symbolized by the icon of the doctor, bishop, professor, or father who knows best—is the breeding ground of abuse by women as well as men.*

The experience with Elizabeth sharpened my perception of how uncritically the concept of boundaries is being used today among many women therapists, especially those working with survivors of childhood sexual abuse. Furthermore, those most involved in efforts to curb sexual abuse by therapists and clergy often tend to absolutize boundaries as walls that discourage intimacy of any sort between professionals and those with whom we work. This absolutizing of boundaries serves to reinforce the abusive logic upon which the healing professions have been structured in the first place—that is, to hold patriarchal power in place.

But there is a pastoral caveat here: as ethically precarious as an *uncritical* use of boundaries is, the fact is that, in hetero/sexist racist patriarchy, the boundaries—that is, *bodily integrity*—of most women, children, and oppressed men have indeed been violated, and our ethics must be grounded in a shared commitment to bring an end to the conditions that generate such violence. Many of my students are struggling courageously in therapy, with friends, and in Twelve-Step programs to develop good—safe, empowering—boundaries. My critique of rigid boundaries, as well as my interest in finding other ways to image ourselves in right-relation—ways that illuminate primarily our connectedness rather than our separateness—should not take precedence in my work over my students' legitimate needs to experience my classes and my professional presence as trustworthy. It is, after all, only *in the relation* between and among ourselves—students and teachers, clients and therapists, sisters and brothers—that we can find our truths about intimacy, safety, risk, or boundaries.

The therapist, the teacher, the priest, or other helper does not ever "know what is best" outside the complex relational dynamic that includes the presence and voices of those who seek professional help. The therapy experience allowed me to understand that it is essential, not optional, for us to work collaboratively not only with professional peers whose values we trust, but also with those who turn to us for help in our professional roles. We cannot know when either the rules of our trade or our intentions are on a collision course with how others are experiencing what we are doing. To be ethical in our work, we need to find nondefensive, creative ways of receiving this evaluative information, ways that are mutually empowering for us and those who are critical of our work. Again, we can only find such ways *together*—with our professional peers and with those who seek our help.

Neither our good intentions and best efforts, nor the rules of our professions, are adequate ethical criteria for our work. We cannot know either abstractly or individually what may be the best, most ethical direction for us to take in a professional situation. *Our ethics, to be genuinely compassionate, must be shaped in ongoing relational processes of dialogue, action, evaluation, and revision.*

ON SHAME AND LIBERATION

I cannot close this book without confessing how *embarrassed* I have been for five years about my therapy pain and obsession. I make this confession not because I believe I have been wrong, silly, or self-indulgent in this preoccupation, or because I believe that I need to be in some way pardoned, except by myself. I make this confession because it strikes me that, through this psychospiritual turmoil, something happened in me, and to me, that has helped me realize how *deeply and fully* creaturely/human we are: I am. Elizabeth is. My students are. We all are, with our broken bodies, our frayed edges, our passions and fears, our hopes and disillusions, and our strong debilitating senses of embarrassment—really, our shame—about the fullness of our deeply human ways of being ourselves in the world. So, I confess some shame about the profoundly creaturely character of these pages. I trust that my creatureliness, that of Elizabeth, and that of all the other characters in these pages reflects something about the *sacred/divine* character of who we all are as sisters, brothers, and friends.

Let me say a little more: I have wrestled with the privilege of spending five years preoccupied with "personal growth." But why have I been ashamed of this? Have I been ashamed of the privilege that has accrued through my race and class locations? Have I been ashamed to have friends and resources—including time, energy, and space in my life—to attend so intensely to this work of personal healing? Have I not realized that friendship, and other resources for healing, are *not* luxuries? Have I not seen that, like food, water, health care, and other sources of life, friendship and the time and space to heal from wounds of whatever sort should be available to all of us?

I have known that, as our economic and social order is structured, time and space and energy are economic commodities, and that we have them (more accurately, we buy them) to the degree that we can afford them. In this sense, I have been mindful of the class (and, in this culture, race) privilege that inheres in these pages. I have also been aware that, without some class privilege, I wouldn't have been in psychotherapy in the first place. And I have been, in this sense, ashamed of myself, ashamed of my privilege.

One of the most troubling, embarrassing aspects of this period has been my feeling stuck, day by day, month after month, in a place of inner turmoil, preoccupied with myself in a way that has seemed often to have little to do with the larger struggle for justice in the world, society, and the church. I've known intellectually that it's all connected. My confidence in this has been secured at the meeting place of liberation spirituality and radical social analysis. But this heady assurance has been small comfort in those moments in which I've been met by bewildered voices, usually *inside* myself, though sometimes those of family and friends:

"What on earth has happened to you, Carter?"

"How could one brief, professional relationship have done this?"

"What difference does this little relationship make in the larger scheme of things?"

"How could you have given so much power to Elizabeth?"

"Can't you see that it was just a 'bad fit,' a relationship that didn't work because you two were philosophically incompatible?"

"What keeps you from just shaking the dust off your feet and getting on with it?"

Through the most difficult period of the healing process—in the two years following the therapy—I didn't know the answers to these questions, and this lack of clarity was intensifying my pain. I wanted so badly to understand, to know what was happening and why. I wanted to understand how this one small relational gestalt was connected to the larger pattern not only of my life but of the social order, the world around Elizabeth and me. I was obsessed with studying the spiritual politics of this matter, with exploring how our relational power, its use and abuse between us, had been formed and de-formed by the world around us.

The only "languages" I could find to help me in this study were in the relational psychology being developed by the Stone Center at Wellesley College and the feminist liberation theology I have been helping to generate with expanding numbers of sisters and brothers. Each of these "languages" was helpful to me, but only in a limited way. The Stone Center, at the time, had developed neither an explicit critique of psychotherapy nor an analysis of power beyond the gender relations of the dominant class and race in western culture. And the feminist liberation theology being done at the Episcopal Divinity School and other centers of progressive theological education reflected little interest on the whole in depth psychology, psychodynamics, psychotherapy, or spirituality as personal journeying.

My personal crisis was to provide a vocational opportunity for me to work with Jan Surrey, Judy Jordan, and others at the Stone Center toward developing therapeutic implications of their own theory. Working with these gifted and courageous women has given me a chance to work on and speak about, as intelligently and constructively as possible, the politics, spirituality, and ethics of psychotherapy as a social institution, both in relation to the larger world and with regard to the relationship between therapist and client. This professional association has provided occasions for me to hear from clinicians and clients about their own therapeutic impasses, ruptures, and woundings; about possibilities for relational healing; and about their commitments to be involved, through their professional work, in the struggles for liberation and justice. I have been able to experience my own experience as instructive and empowering to others, and this has been empowering and healing for me. My work with the Stone Center has helped lift the shame from me.

It's been as a feminist liberation theologian that my embarrassment has been most acute, for what in the world have I been thinking about, focusing so narrowly on psychotherapy—indeed, on my own experience—as a primary location of spiritual and theological import? Whoever could imagine that a feminist liberation theologian would devote so much energy over a five-year period to, and write a book on, her psychotherapy—my questions, projected outward.

Embarrassment is an emotional by-product of *shame,* and shame is a psychospiritual burden we carry insofar as we do not believe that we are basically good and creative, lovable and capable earthcreatures worthy of profound respect. And what is the vision and goal of all theology worth if not to encourage, as concretely as possible, the creation of conditions in the world (society, cultures, religions, professions, and so forth) through which *all* of us can better realize that we are basically good and creative, lovable and capable creatures worthy of respect?

I have been ashamed of myself for struggling so hard to understand why I was so wounded—so *shamed*—through the therapy experience! I have been ashamed of myself especially as a feminist liberation theologian.

But why? Do I believe that feminists, or theologians, are above being shamed? No.

So why? Do I assume that feminist liberation theologians should be above dealing with our personal shame in our professional work, using theology as a vehicle for personal growth rather than as an articulation of a larger, more communal commitment? Do I, like most white western christian theologians, at some level accept the patriarchal logic of a lingering opposition and a hierarchy of value between public and private, larger and smaller, communal and individual, intellectual and emotional life?

Have I been ashamed of myself because, for five years, I have feared that my theological focus has not been "big," "important," or, in that sense, "political" enough? Is Sophie not enough of a feminist? Have I not been a reliable feminist sister? Have I been in so much psychospiritual turmoil as to be ineffective in the larger struggles? These questions have been mine, originating in a place of embarrassment about being a fully human sister who, like all earthcreatures, reflects the vulnerability and passion of God.

And in those moments when I've been most grounded in our sacred relational power—through Twelve-Step participation, meditation, friendship, teaching, playing with the animals, walking, writing, feeling deeply and thinking well, acting politically, making love—the expectation that I should, or can, be anything other than a fully human being, an awkward, vibrant creature, has been lifted from me.

In that sacred moment, I accept the pain, the "smallness" of this particular passion, the embarrassment, and this strange painful journey as part of a whole—connected and significant, even if not fully clear to me or others. I accept this and as I do, I hear a voice deep in my soul:

There is in each of us a need to be heard to speech. A need born in our souls, the place of all real meeting, in which every I-Thou and all unalienated erotic power is conceived. This need in each of us is not a pathology. It is not a weakness. It is not a sin. The need does not originate in abuse. Its roots are not shameful. It is not immature. This need is not something to be treated or healed, liberated or outgrown. It is something in each of us to be cultivated and cherished, experienced and shared, with respect and tenderness, awe and humor.

There is in each of us a need to be heard to speech. It is a need to recognize, name, and celebrate our connectedness, a need that can be met only through radical mutuality. This need is so strong and so seldom met that it becomes an obsession from which there is, finally, no escape. If we deny it, we fossilize and learn to live without living. If we accept it, we become more fully creaturely creative—and, in so doing, learn to suffer together, because we cannot love one another without suffering with one another the sins of the world that gladly would extinguish this need of ours, to be heard to speech.

There is in each of us a need to be heard to speech. This need is the root of all genuine healing and the source of all creative revolutionary movement. It is the wellspring of our redemption, and it is the hope of the world.

Afterword (Foreword, 1993)

Janet L. Surrey

THIS BOOK CHRONICLES an agonizing and ultimately liberating passage through a therapy relationship. The juxtaposition of real healing and terrible wounding within this relationship is described by Carter Heyward with a degree of personal exposure and vulnerability that those of us who know her work have come to respect as the wellspring of her bold theology, her sharp and seasoned political wisdom, her confrontation with real-life ethics, and ultimately her extraordinary capacity for friendship.

The chronicle of this therapy is highly personal and particular yet speaks to the possibilities of such wounding within any dyadic relationship isolated within the context of families, professions, institutions, and organizations rooted in patriarchal "power-over" structures. It is recognizable to all of us as clients, therapists, friends, partners, and coworkers. The challenge of this book is to move us beyond the personal, to challenge our individualistic thinking, and to name the primary problem as beyond any individual's "issues" or personal limits.

The liberating energies of this journey—of moving fully *into* and *not away from* the heart of healing and abuse within relationship— suggest a journey of faith and transformation of resounding depth. Through this journey, the roots and branches of Carter Heyward's relational theology of liberation are more fully revealed.

Carter's passionate nature and spirit, her refusal to go "numb" or to avoid or doubt the truth of her experience, challenges us all to examine ever more carefully and painstakingly the common roots of our suffering in relationships and the real source of true healing and liberation in our lives. From there, we can begin to create and live into new forms and dynamics of healing.

There is nothing more moving to me in this book than Carter's description of her own healing circle of friends, created not fully consciously, yet artfully, to move with her through and beyond her pain. Her inclusion of many of our voices within this book reflects how deeply interconnected and essential we are to each other and is a testimony to our capacity to share our pain so that it is bearable, to use our experience to comprehend our world, and to work together to revision and reshape that world. The power of such a circle of women friends has yet to be made fully visible and recognized for its healing and liberating potential. All of us have grown and moved in our lives and work through the sharing of Carter's struggle.

My friendship with Carter was shaped by our deeply shared reverence for the creative and healing energies of relationship. Our work together has supported and enlarged my own thinking as a feminist psychologist and theorist in appreciating the implications of a theological, ethical, and political analysis of the context of our lives and the institutions within which we live and work.

As a friend, I have suffered with, struggled with, and learned with Carter and have felt privileged to be entrusted with her confidence. As a psychologist, I have been deeply moved. I have felt pain for Carter and empathy for Elizabeth Farro, her therapist. Elizabeth's decision to hold on to the traditional structure of individual psychotherapy probably made it impossible for her to respond with the passion and intensity Carter asks of her. The temptation to frame this as either individual's failure or "pathology" is an easy, too habitual way of *not* seeing the limits and constraints and, at times, consequences of our practice within traditional orthodox structures. I can identify with each of these women and recognize the contradictions and troubling implications of our currently defined professional "ethics" and standards. I feel anguish for the lack of Elizabeth's voice in this work. As Carter has said, the full truth can be realized only when all involved are able to speak and to question together the larger context. Both Elizabeth's silence and Carter's voice "speak" for us and reflect our struggles as therapists and clients and teachers and clergy and health professionals to live successfully in our world and at the same time to experience the authenticity and mutuality of true relationship, which is the core of our lives and healing.

Janet L. Surrey

Janet L. Surrey is a clinical psychologist, a psychotherapist in private practice, and a Project Consultant and Research Associate at the Stone Center for Development Services and Studies at Wellesley College. She is a co-author of Women's Growth in Connection: Writings from the Stone Center *(New York: Guilford Press, 1991), and, with Stephen Bergman, has initiated the Center for Gender Relations.*

Notes

FOREWORD

1. John McKnight, *The Careless Society: Community and Its Counterfeits* (New York: Basic Books, 1995), 16.

2. Ibid., 16.

3. Pamela Cooper-White et al., "Desperately Seeking Sophia's Shadow," *Journal of Pastoral Care* 48 (fall 1994): 287-92; Carrie Doehring, *Taking Care: Monitoring Power Dynamics and Relational Boundaries in Pastoral Care and Counseling* (Nashville: Abingdon Press, 1995), 172 n. 14; Marie M. Fortune, review of *When Boundaries Betray Us: Beyond Illusions of What Is Ethical in Therapy and Life*, by Carter Heyward, *Christian Century* (18-25 May 1994): 524-26; Fortune, "Response to Heyward's Response," *Christian Century* (1-8 June 1994): 579-82; Christie Cozad Neuger, review of *When Boundaries Betray Us: Beyond Illusions of What Is Ethical in Therapy and Life*, by Carter

Heyward, *Princeton Seminary Bulletin* 16:3 (1995): 381–84; K. Roberts Skerrett, "When No Means Yes: The Passion of Carter Heyward," *Journal of Feminist Studies in Religion* 12:1 (spring 1996): 71–92.

4. McKnight, *The Careless Society,* 16.

5. Cooper-White et al., "Desperately Seeking," 287–92; Doehring, *Taking Care,* 172 n. 14; Fortune, review of *When Boundaries Betray Us*; Fortune, "Response to Heyward's Response"; Neuger, review of *When Boundaries Betray Us*; Skerrett, "When No Means Yes," 71–92.

6. Bruce E. Bennett et al., *Professional Liability and Risk Management* (Washington, D.C.: American Psychological Association, 1990), 119, 40, 35; Roy Herndon SteinhoffSmith "The Boundary Wars Mystery," *Religious Studies Review* 24:2 (April 1998): 131–42, 133.

7. Fortune, review of *When Boundaries Betray Us.*

8. Doehring, *Taking Care,* 172 n. 14.

9. Neuger, review of *When Boundaries Betray Us*; Skerrett, "When No Means Yes."

10. Roy Herndon SteinhoffSmith, *The Mutuality of Care* (St. Louis: Chalice Press, 1999), 20.

11. Carter Heyward, *Staying Power: Reflections on Gender, Justice, and Compassion* (Cleveland: The Pilgrim Press, 1995), 9.

12. SteinhoffSmith, *The Mutuality of Care*, 20.

13. SteinhoffSmith, "The Boundary Wars Mystery," 135.

14. Fortune, *Love Does No Harm: Sexual Ethics for the Rest of Us* (New York: Continuum, 1995), 31–32.

15. SteinhoffSmith, *The Mutuality of Care.*, 20.

16. Fortune, *Love Does No Harm*, 28.

17. Ibid., 42–44.

18. SteinhoffSmith, "The Boundary Wars Mystery."

19. Ibid.

20. Ibid.

21. Fortune, *Love Does No Harm.*

22. Anne Bathurst Gilson, *Eros Breaking Free: Interpreting Sexual Theo-Ethics* (Cleveland: The Pilgrim Press, 1995), 59–61.

23. Fortune, "Review of Carter Heyward."

24. SteinhoffSmith, "The Boundary Wars Mystery."

25. Donald Capps, *The Child's Song: The Religious Abuse of Children* (Louisville: Westminster John Knox, 1995), 6–20.

26. Cooper-White et al., "Desperately Seeking"; Doehring, *Taking Care,* 172 n. 14; Fortune, review of *When Boundaries Betray Us*; Neuger, review of *When Boundaries Betray Us*; Skerrett, "When No Means Yes."

27. Doehring, *Taking Care,* 172 n. 14.

28. Fortune, review of *When Boundaries Betray Us.*

29. Skerrett, "When No Means Yes," 83.

30. Ibid., 74.

31. Ibid., 75.

32. Ibid., 75–76.

33. Ibid., 90–91.

34. Ibid., 73.

35. Ibid., 89–90.

36. Heyward, *The Redemption of God: A Theology of Mutual Relation* (Lanham, Md.: University Press of America, 1982), 20.

37. SteinhoffSmith, "The Boundary Wars Mystery," 141.

INTRODUCTION

1. I use the word "strata" rather than "class" so as not to obscure the actual class structure in America at this time: at the top are 1 to 2 percent of the population who constitute a tiny ownership class and another 20 percent who are a professional managerial class. At the much larger bottom are the working class, including the working poor and the underemployed and the unemployed. Between the top and bottom of the class structure are people in the fluid "middle strata," who increasingly are working class yet think of themselves as "middle class" and, therefore, as upwardly mobile. In other words, in our political economy, there really is no "middle class" but rather people in class transition—moving either up or, much more often, down, yet who often fail to see that this is the case. The term "middle class" obscures the reality of our fluid, and downward, mobility.

2. By *erotic*, I mean our creative life force, our sacred Spirit. See Audre Lorde, "Uses of the Erotic: The Erotic as Power," *Sister Outsider: Essays and Speeches* (Trumansburg, N.Y.: Crossing Press, 1984); Heyward, *Touching Our Strength: The Erotic as Power and the Love of God* (San Francisco: Harper & Row, 1989); and Rita Nakashima Brock, *Journeys by Heart: A Christology of Erotic Power* (New York: Crossroad Press, 1988).

3. See Nelle Morton, *The Journey Is Home* (Boston: Beacon Press, 1985), 202–10.

4. See, for example, Elisabeth Schüssler Fiorenza, *In Memory of Her* (New York: Crossroad, 1984), and Susan Cady, Marian Ronan, and Hal Taussig, *Wisdom's Feast* (San Francisco: HarperSanFrancisco, 1989), on Sophia. Increasing numbers of feminist scholars of christianity suggest that the female Sophia was displaced in early christianity by the christic-messianic character bestowed upon the man Jesus in the centuries immediately following his life and death and the resurrection experience of his disciples. The cause and effect of Sophia's displacement and trivialization in christianity has been christian misogyny and the ongoing oppression of women in the church and in the larger society, with the church's blessing.

PART 1

1. Reference is to a dream I had about meeting Elizabeth at the Bread and Circus market in Cambridge.

2. In the fall of 1988 Jan Surrey and I co-taught a course at the Episcopal Divinity School entitled "Theology and Psychology: Conversations." In the spring of 1989 I gave a presentation at the Stone Center, "Coming Out as Relational Empowerment: A Lesbian Feminist Theological Perspective." In the spring of 1990 Jan and I taught a course, "Women, Addiction, and Empowerment," at EDS, and in February 1991 we led a workshop on addiction at the school. In the summer of 1990, at Laura S. Brown's invitation, we participated on a panel on feminist ethics at the convention of the American Psychological Association. In the spring of 1991 Katie G. Cannon and I made a presentation, "Alienation and Anger: A Black Woman's and a White Woman's Struggle for Mutuality in an Unjust World," at the Stone Center. In the fall of 1991 Jan and I taught "Relationship, Abuse, and Healing" at EDS, and in the spring of 1992 we collaborated with Judith V. Jordan on a Stone Center Colloquium presentation, "Mutuality in Therapy: Ethics, Power, and Psychology." We have also led workshops on addiction and empowerment and on mutuality in therapy at the Harvard Medical School/Cambridge Hospital/Stone Center's annual Conference on Women. In the fall semester of 1993, with William Rankin, I taught a course at EDS, "Non-Violence as a Relational Way: Theological, Ethical, and Psychological Dimensions."

3. For more on what I mean by mutuality, see especially Heyward, *The Redemption of God* and *Touching Our Strength*..

PART 2

1. Little Rye is an island in Maine's Penobscot Bay where I spent three days alone in 1988.

2. Robert and Isabel are my nephew and niece; Teraph was my aging dog.

3. Heyward, *Touching Our Strength*.

4. Adrienne Rich, "Women and Honor: Some Notes on Lying," in *On Lies, Secrets, and Silence: Selected Prose 1966-1978* (New York: W. W. Norton, 1979), 194.

5. For this reason, I did not dedicate *Touching Our Strength* to her.

6. Heyward, "Coming Out and Relational Empowerment: A Lesbian Feminist Theological Perspective," Work in Progress no. 38 (Wellesley, Mass.: Stone Center for Developmental Services and Studies, 1989).

7. This gathering is called the 10% of Us Conference.

8. See Beverly W. Harrison's essay in *Making the Connections: Essays in Feminist Social Ethics*, ed. Carol S. Robb (Boston: Beacon Press, 1985); and

Donna Haraway, *Simians, Cyborgs, and Women: The Reinvention of Nature* (New York: Routledge, 1990).

9. Heyward, "Suffering, Redemption, and Christ: A Review," *Christianity and Crisis* 49, no. 17/18 (11 December 1989): 381–86.

10. Heyward, "The Power of God-with-Us," How My Mind Has Changed Series, *Christian Century* 107, no. 9 (14 March 1990): 275–78.

11. See Heyward, *The Redemption of God*, chap. 4.

12. See Charles William, *Descent into Hell* (New York: Pelligrini and Cudahy, 1949); and Martin Buber, *I and Thou* (New York: Scribners, 1958).

13. See, for example, Brock, *Journeys by Heart:*; Chung Hyun Kyung, *Struggle to Be the Sun Again: Introducing Asian Women's Theology* (Maryknoll, N.Y.: Orbis Books, 1990); Heyward, *The Redemption of God*; Heyward, *Our Passion for Justice: Images of Power, Sexuality, and Liberation* (New York: The Pilgrim Press, 1984); Ada María Isasi-Díaz and Yolanda Tarango, *Hispanic Women: Prophetic Voice in the Church* (Minneapolis: Fortress Press, 1988); The Mudflower Collective, *God's Fierce Whimsy: Christian Feminism and Theological Education* (New York: The Pilgrim Press, 1985); Rosemary Radford Ruether, *Sexism and God-Talk: Toward a Feminist Theology* (Boston: Beacon Press, 1983); Susan B. Thistlethwaite and Mary P. Engel, *Lift Every Voice: Constructing Christian Theologies from the Underside* (San Francisco: HarperSanFrancisco, 1990); Sharon Welch, *Communities of Resistance and Solidarity* (Maryknoll, N.Y.: Orbis Books, 1985); and Delores S. Williams, *Sisters in the Wilderness: The Challenge of Womanist God-Talk* (Maryknoll, N.Y.: Orbis Books, 1993).

14. See Judith V. Jordan, Alexandra Kaplan, Jean Baker Miller, Irene P. Stiver, and Janet L. Surrey, *Woman's Growth in Connection: Writings from the Stone Center* (New York: Guilford Press, 1991); see also the Works in Progress papers from the Stone Center for Developmental Services and Studies (Wellesley College, Wellesley, Mass.)

15. Our ideas were presented as an *outline* on a panel on Feminist Ethics and Psychology at the American Psychological Association's annual meeting in August 1990; as a *workshop* at the Harvard Medical School/Cambridge Hospital/Stone Center Conference on Women in spring 1991; as a *Stone Center Colloquium presentation*, with Judith V. Jordan in March 1992; and as a *Stone Center workshop* in October 1992.

16. Peg Huff, Chris Blackburn, Darlene Nicrogski, Janie VanZandt, Anne Gilson, Norene Carter, Karen Whittsley-First, Alison Cheek, and Heather Weihl were the sisters gathered with Bev, Teraph, and me.

17. See Harrison, "The Power of Anger," in *Making the Connections.*

18. Miriam Greenspan, *A New Approach to Women and Therapy*, 2d ed. (New York: Tab Books/McGraw-Hill, 1993).

19. For an adaptation of this lecture see the Appendix to the 1993 edition of this book.

20. Back in Cambridge for the spring semester in 1991, I began teaching a christology seminar in which one of the students, Mariel Kinsey, was working on a contemporary interpretation of the Sumerian myth of Inanna and Erishkigal, in which Erishkigal hangs her sister, Inanna, on a meat hook to die when Inanna journeys into the underworld to find and rescue her. The story generated much conversation in class about horizontal violence among women, and how we wound one another out of ignorance, jealousy—so many motives, but primarily fear.

21. Angela, a life-professed member of the Community of St. Clare in Stroud, New South Wales, Australia, is also a renowned sculptor who works in wood and bronze. She was ordained to the priesthood of the Anglican Church on December 21, 1992.

PART 3

1. Heyward, *The Redemption of God*.

Selected
Readings (1993)

Author's note: I have not attempted to update this section. For an expanded bibliography, including a number of essays written in response to the 1993 publication of *When Boundaries Betray Us*, see notes and bibliographical resources in Roy Herndon SteinhoffSmith, *The Mutuality of Care* (St. Louis: Chalice Press, 1999).

Belenky, M. F.; Clinchy, B. M.; Goldberger, N. R.; and Tarule, J. M. *Women's Ways of Knowing: The Development of Self, Voice, and Mind.* New York: Basic Books, 1986.

Brown, L. S. "Beyond Thou Shalt Not: Thinking About Ethics in the Lesbian Therapy Community." *Women and Therapy: A Feminist Quarterly* 8, no. 1/2 (Spring/Summer 1988): 13–25.

———. "Not Outside the Range: One Feminist Perspective on Psychic Trauma." *American Imago* 48, no. 1 (Spring 1991): 119–33.

Buber, M. *I and Thou.* New York: Scribners, 1958.

Cannon, K. G., and Heyward, C. "Alienation and Anger: A Black Woman's and a White Woman's Struggle for Mutuality in an Unjust World." Work in Progress no. 54. Wellesley, MA: Stone Center, 1991.

Dallett, J. O. *When the Spirits Come Back.* Toronto: Inner City Books, 1983.

Gilligan, C. *In a Different Voice: Psychological Theory and Women's Development.* Cambridge: Harvard Univ. Press, 1982.

Gilligan, C.; Lyons, N. P.; and Hanmer, T. J., eds. *Making Connections: The Relational Worlds of Adolescent Girls at Emma Willard School.* Troy, NY: Emma Willard, 1989.

Gilligan, C.; Rogers, A. G.; and Tollman, D. L. *Women, Girls and Psychotherapy: Reframing Resistance.* New York: Harrington Park Press, 1991.

Gottlieb, R. "Masculine Identity and the Desire for War." In *Rethinking Power,* edited by Thomas E. Wartenberg, 277–88. Albany: State Univ. of New York Press, 1992.

Greenspan, M. *A New Approach to Women and Therapy.* 2d ed. New York: Tab Books/McGraw-Hill, 1993.

———. "Should Therapists Be Personal? Self-Disclosure and Therapeutic Distance in Feminist Therapy." *Women and Therapy: A Feminist Quarterly* 5, no. 2/3 (Summer/Fall 1986; special issue on the dynamics of feminist therapy, edited by Doris Howard): 5–17.

Grey, M. *Redeeming the Dream: Feminism, Redemption, and Christian Tradition.* London: SPCK, 1989.

Grof, S., and Bennett, H. Z. *The Holotropic Mind: The Three Levels of Human Consciousness and How They Shape Our Lives.* San Francisco: HarperSanFrancisco, 1992.

Habermas, J. *Theory and Practice.* Boston: Beacon Press, 1973.

Hanley-Hackenbruck, P. "Working with Lesbians in Psychotherapy." *American Psychiatric Press Review of Psychiatry* 12 (1993): 59–93.

Haraway, D. *Simians, Cyborgs, and Women: The Reinvention of Nature.* New York: Routledge, 1990.

Harrison, B. W. "The Power of Anger in the Work of Love." In *Making the Connections: Essays in Feminist Social Ethics,* edited by Carol S. Robb, 2–21. Boston: Beacon Press, 1985.

Heyward, C. *The Redemption of God: A Theology of Mutual Relation.* Lanham, MD: Univ. Press of America, 1982.

———. *Touching Our Strength: The Erotic as Power and the Love of God.* San Francisco: Harper and Row, 1989.

———. "Coming Out and Relational Empowerment: A Lesbian Feminist Theological Perspective." Work in Progress no. 38. Wellesley, MA: Stone Center, 1989.

Heyward, C.; Jordan, J.; and Surrey, J. "Mutuality in Therapy: Ethics, Power and Psychology." Work in Progress. Wellesley, MA: Stone Center, 1993.

Hoagland, S. L. *Lesbian Ethics: Toward New Value.* Palo Alto, CA: Institute of Lesbian Studies, 1988.

Huff, M. C. "The Interdependent Self: An Integrated Concept from Feminist Theology and Feminist Psychology." *Philosophy and Theology* 2, no. 2 (Winter 1987): 160–72.

Hunt, M. E. *Fierce Tenderness: Toward a Feminist Theology of Friendship.* New York: Crossroad, 1991.

James, W. *The Varieties of Religious Experience: A Study in Human Nature.* New York: New American Library, Mentor Books, 1958.

Jordan, J. V. "Clarity in Connection: Empathic Knowing, Desire, and Sexuality." Work in Progress no. 29. Wellesley, MA: Stone Center, 1987.

———. "Relational Development: Therapeutic Implications of Empathy and Shame." Work in Progress no. 39. Wellesley, MA: Stone Center, 1989.

———. "Courage in Connection" Work in Progress no. 45. Wellesley, MA: Stone Center, 1990.

———. "The Movement of Mutuality and Power." Work in Progress no. 53. Wellesley, MA: Stone Center, 1990.

———. "Relational Resilience." Work in Progress no. 57. Wellesley, MA: Stone Center, 1991.

Jordan, J. V.; Kaplan, A. G.; Miller, J. B.; Stiver, I. P.; and Surrey, J. L. *Women's Growth in Connection: Writings from the Stone Center.* New York: Guilford Press, 1991.

Kaschak, E. *Engendered Lives: A New Psychology of Women's Experience.* New York: Basic Books, 1992.

Laidlaw, T. A.; Malmo, C.; and Associates. *Healing Voices: Feminist Approaches to Therapy with Women.* San Francisco: Jossey-Bass, 1990.

Laing, R. D. *The Politics of Experience.* New York: Ballantine Books, 1967.

Lorde, A. "Uses of the Erotic: The Erotic as Power." In *Sister Outsider: Essays and Speeches,* 53–59. Trumansburg, NY: Crossing Press, 1984.

Lukoff, D.; Turner, R.; and Lu, F. "Transpersonal Psychology Research Review: Psychoreligious Dimensions of Healing." *Journal of Transpersonal Psychology* 24, no. 1 (1992): 41–60.

Lykes, M. B. "Gender and Individualistic vs. Collectivist Bases for Notions About the Self." *Journal of Personality* 53, no. 2 (1985): 357–83.

Lyons, N. P. "Two Perspectives: On Self, Relationships, and Morality." *Harvard Educational Review* 52, no. 2 (1983): 125–45.

Miller, J. B. *Toward a New Psychology of Women.* 2d ed. Boston: Beacon Press, 1986.

———. "Connections, Disconnections, and Violations." Work in Progress no. 33. Wellesley, MA: Stone Center, 1988.

Miller, J. B.; Jordan, J. V.; Kaplan, A. G.; Stiver, I. P.; and Surrey, J. L. "Some Misconceptions and Reconceptions of a Relational Approach." Work in Progress no. 49. Wellesley, MA: Stone Center, 1990.

Miller, J. B., and Stiver, I. P. "A Relational Reframing of Therapy." Work in Progress no. 52. Wellesley, MA: Stone Center, 1991.

Morton, N. *The Journey Is Home.* Boston: Beacon Press, 1985.

Rich, A. "Women and Honor: Some Notes on Lying." In *On Lies, Secrets, and Silence: Selected Prose, 1966–1978*, 185–94. New York: W. W. Norton, 1979.

Spelman, E. V. *Inessential Woman: Problems of Exclusion in Feminist Thought.* Boston: Beacon Press, 1988.

Starhawk. *Truth or Dare: Encounters with Power, Authority, and Mystery.* San Francisco: Harper and Row, 1987.

Stiver, I. P. "A Relational Approach to Therapeutic Impasses." Work in Progress no. 58. Wellesley, MA: Stone Center, 1991.

Sullivan, H. S. *The Interpersonal Theory of Psychiatry.* New York: W. W. Norton, 1953.

Surrey, J. L. "Relationship and Empowerment." Work in Progress no. 30. Wellesley, MA: Stone Center, 1987.

Thakar, V. *Songs of Yearning.* Berkeley, CA: Vimala Programs (P.O. Box 657), 1983.

———. *Spirituality and Social Action: A Holistic Approach.* Berkeley, CA: Vimala Programs (P.O. Box 657), 1984.

Thich Nhat Hanh. *The Miracle of Mindfulness! A Manual on Meditation.* Boston: Beacon Press, 1975.

———. *The Sun My Heart: From Mindfulness to Insight Contemplation.* Berkeley: Parallax, 1988.

Valle, R. S. "The Emergence of Transpersonal Psychology." In *Existential Phenomenological Perspectives in Psychology*, edited by R. S. Valle and S. Halling, 257–68. New York: Plenum, 1989.

Van der Kolk, B. *Psychological Trauma.* Washington, DC: American Psychiatric Press, 1987.

Wehr, D. *Jung and Feminism: Liberating Archetypes.* Boston: Beacon Press, 1987.

Welch, S. D. *Communities of Resistance and Solidarity.* Maryknoll, NY: Orbis Books, 1985.

———. *A Feminist Ethics of Risk.* Minneapolis: Fortress Press, 1990.

Weston, A. "The Wounded Healer: Power and Vulnerability in the Psychotherapy Relationship." Paper presented at the Saturday Seminar Series, Berkeley, CA, 1989.

Wikse, C. V. *About Possession: The Self as Private Property.* University Park: Pennsylvania State Univ. Press, 1977.

Williams, C. *Descent into Hell.* New York: Pelligrini and Cudahy, 1949.

Young, W. "Psychodynamics and Dissociation: All That Switches Is Not Split." *Dissociation* 1 (1983): 13–20.